About Leadership Network

The mission of Leadership Network is to accelerate the emergence of effective churches by identifying and connecting innovative church leaders, providing them with resources in the form of new ideas, people, and tools, and communicating its learnings to the broader church. Churches and church leaders served by Leadership Network represent a wide variety of primarily Protestant faith traditions that range from mainline to evangelical to independent. They are characterized by innovation, entrepreneurial leadership, and a desire to be on the cutting edge of ministry.

While Leadership Network was founded on and remains guided by the core tenets of Biblical faith, its focus has been on the practice and application of faith at the local congregational level. It believes the emerging paradigm of the twenty-first century church calls for the development of a new type of church leader, both clergy and laity, who can lead the transition from an institution-based church to a mission-driven church.

Leadership Network is a network of networks that reflects both the diversity and scope of its mission. The four core networks include

- the Large Church Network, that fosters peer learning at forums, conferences, and special learning events
- the Church Champions Network, that focuses on the practical application of the learnings at the local church level through consultants, regional denominational leaders, and teaching churches
- the Young Leader Network, that connects those doing ministry within the Emerging Culture
- the Information Network, that explores the future and disseminates the learnings of the other networks through publications, fax services, and websites

A sister organization, the Leadership Training Network, uses peer learning and interactive training to accelerate the lay mobilization movement and gift-based team ministry.

Established as a private foundation in 1984 by social entrepreneur Bob Buford, Leadership Network is acknowledged as an influential leader among churches and parachurch ministries, and a major resource that innovative church leaders turn to for networking and information.

If you would like additional information on Leadership Network, please contact them directly:
Leadership Network, 2501 Cedar Springs, Suite 200, Dallas, Texas 75201. Telephone: (800) 765-5323. Fax: (214) 969-9392.
E-mail: info@leadnet.org   Website: www.leadnet.org

Leading the
Team-Based Church

LEADING THE TEAM-BASED CHURCH

How Pastors and Church Staffs Can Grow Together into a Powerful Fellowship of Leaders

George Cladis

A Publication of Leadership Network

Jossey-Bass Publishers
San Francisco

Credits are on p. 191.

Jossey-Bass books and products are available through most bookstores. To contact Jossey-Bass directly, call (888) 378-2537, fax to (800) 605-2665, or visit our website at www.josseybass.com.

Substantial discounts on bulk quantities of Jossey-Bass books are available to corporations, professional associations, and other organizations. For details and discount information, contact the special sales department at Jossey-Bass.

Manufactured in the United States of America on Lyons Falls Turin Book. This paper is acid-free and 100 percent totally chlorine-free.

Library of Congress Cataloging-in-Publication Data

Cladis, George, date.
 Leading the team-based church: how pastors and church staffs can grow together into a powerful fellowship of leaders / George Cladis. — 1st ed.
  p. cm. — (The Jossey-Bass religion-in-practice series)
 Includes bibliographical references and index.
 ISBN 0-7879-4119-0 (alk. paper)
  1. Group ministry. I. Title. II. Series.
BV675.C53 1999
253—dc21   98-40264

FIRST EDITION

HB Printing 10 9 8 7 6 5 4 3

CONTENTS

For Martie, Christopher, Katherine, and Nicholas

My closest circle of love

PREFACE

The Critical Need for Team-Based Churches

AFTER TWENTY YEARS of ministry involving a lot of trial and error, I have come to a rock-solid conviction that has revolutionized my ministry: if a church is to succeed in carrying out a healthy ministry and developing a good Christian community there must be stable and high-quality relationships among the members of the principal leadership team.

A healthy church leadership team with trusting relationships radiates health and vitality throughout the church organization and its whole system of relationships. Just as powerfully, a dysfunctional team radiates pain and dissension throughout the congregation. How those responsible for church leadership lead staff or ministry boards and teams has an enormous effect on the quality of relationships within the church community and the congregation's effectiveness in ministry. This book focuses on practical ways to build a strong leadership team that becomes the model team to the rest of the congregation, keeps the church focused and directed in healthy ways, and inspires others to team ministry.

Team-based ministry is the most effective model for leading and organizing Christian ministry for the twenty-first century. There has never been a more important time for the Church of Jesus Christ to be led by sincere, dedicated teams of disciples who labor together in God's fellowship to live the Gospel in a turbulent world. *Leading the Team-Based Church* presents a biblical and theological model that can be the foundation for structuring congregations around ministry teams. From this model I derive very practical ways to form a leadership team that models collaborative teamwork to the congregation and inspires the creation of additional teams. A team-based model also fits well with new trends emerging in today's world, the *postmodern* world. I argue that certain aspects of postmodern culture actually encourage the church to make needed reforms; reforms that are foundational to biblical Christianity.

The late twentieth century has been marked by a severe decline in the influence and effectiveness of traditional churches and a sharp rise in new, *entrepreneurial* congregations. The decline represents a crisis in traditional churches that can be summed up in two categories: spiritual and organizational. This book deals mostly with responding to the latter kind of crisis, though the two can hardly be separated. In fact, although I have assumed that interested readers will be spiritually energized and committed Christians, the structuring of congregations around the team model presented here can actually be a catalyst for spiritual renewal. Nonetheless, readers hoping simply to find gimmicks and clever techniques to quickly inspire congregations will be disappointed. This book is for the committed Christian wanting to bring vital faith and church organization closer together to serve effectively the Kingdom of God in a postmodern culture.

I wrote *Leading the Team-Based Church* as a result of my own spiritual journey for meaning in church leadership. My search began with a gnawing conviction that what we read in Scripture and what we believe about Christian community are often not reflected in the church office and board room, let alone the congregation at large. The denominational church models we have inherited are not working. And the frantic searches of independent churches for *grow quick* gimmicks fail miserably to develop enduring churches. We need today strong, steady, biblical, theologically sound, and culturally appropriate models of church leadership *that work*.

My journey led me to this conclusion: the theological model of God as Trinity contains a useful and meaningful model for leading effective churches in today's world. From this model we can derive practical ways to form ministry teams that can transform old, dying congregations into vibrant ministries. Moreover, team ministry is the form of leadership called for both by Christian theology and today's cultural environment.

This book is the result of years of struggle to understand and learn what builds effective congregations in a postmodern world. My search has been difficult. It has been punctuated with failure. It has been shaped by church conflict and staff battles. These events, as disillusioning and heartbreaking as they were, inspired and prompted me to study what makes for good leadership in the church and then to *bring it about*.

Audience

I intend in this book to bridge two communities that need to come closer together. On the one hand, the theological community, dwelling in the realm of ideas and concepts, is currently developing a new interest and fascination with Trinitarian theology. On the other hand, church leaders are wrestling with the very real problems of trying to minister to people living in a culture that has shifted radically in recent years, rendering traditional ministries archaic and ineffective. The theological community likes to *think* about new ways of envisioning God. The church leadership community seeks new ways of *doing* ministry. In this book, I seek to bring together a theological and biblical way of *thinking* about God and a more effective and very practical way of *doing* ministry in a postmodern world.

Therefore, this book will be most helpful to church leaders who are seeking ways of leading that are both theologically sound and effective. Pastors, elders, deacons, and other church leaders will find this book quite helpful. Theologians should be provoked into thinking further about the application of new trends in Trinitarian theology. Leaders of Christian organizations other than churches will find this book helpful because the ideas and methods discussed extend beyond the local church to any faith community seeking to give witness to Christ in today's world.

Overview of the Contents

The chapters in Part One draw out both the theological model that is foundational for team-based ministry and the cultural ethos that makes teams so effective. In Chapter One, I argue that the fellowship (what I will develop as the *perichoresis*) of the three persons of God represents the community we are called to imitate in the church. The Father, Son, and Spirit are a kind of *team* that reveals to us seven attributes of Christian fellowship that make for effective church leadership today. In Chapter Two, I describe how the characteristics of postmodern culture form the context for team-based ministry and how that culture actually can *contribute* to a church's making important changes.

The seven chapters in Part Two discuss the seven attributes of the fellowship of God that characterize a strong leadership team. These chapters present the specific steps congregations and church leaders can take to form a leadership team that reflects these seven attributes (or related characteristics). I argue that a biblically and theologically sound leadership team will be a *covenanting team, visionary team, collaborative team, culture-creating team, trusting team, empowering team,* and *learning team.* A team with these attributes becomes a powerful fellowship of leaders. In addition it becomes the pattern for a whole host of teams, and the chapter on the learning team discusses practical ways to extend the team model throughout the whole congregation and beyond.

Leading the Team-Based Church concludes with an encouraging word that sums up the journey of creating a team-based church.

A Note About Examples

Throughout this book, I have used illustrations from real churches and organizations. When I supply a specific location, the names of the organization and of its people are also the actual names. When a specific location is not supplied, the illustration has been heavily disguised, and names have been changed along with other personal details. Because of these changes, any apparent similarities to situations you know are only coincidental. The First Church of Appleton (also called the Apple Hill Church) is fictitious, though its story is a collage of many true-to-life events from various congregations.

Acknowledgments

I want to thank those who have endured me during the months of writing this book. Martie, my patient and supportive wife, put on hold some projects we do together so I could finish the book. My children, Christopher, Katherine, and Nicholas, gave up a part of their dad for a period of time so I could write.

The people of Covenant Presbyterian Church in Austin, Texas, where I formerly served as pastor and team leader, gave me deep love and affection. Their enduring spirit encouraged and rewarded me in countless ways. And the people of the Noroton Presbyterian Church in Darien, Connecticut, who called me as their new senior pastor in the spring of 1998, gave me the gifts of time and encouragement to finish this work.

My thanks also to Bob Buford, Brad Smith, Travis Davis, and the rest of the Leadership Network team without whose influence this search might never have begun. In addition, clergy friends and conference attendees encouraged me to get this material into writing so it could be reviewed and studied.

Carol Childress of Leadership Network served as general editor for this publication; her friendship, sharp mind, and faithful spirit have been both inspiring and instructive. Sarah Polster, senior editor of the Religion in Practice series at Jossey-Bass, never gave up on me but required my best. She expertly steered me to keep to the *practice* of faith and not just its articulation. Christina Blair, Stanley Hall, and J. Ellis Nelson of Austin Presbyterian Theological Seminary let me change horses midstream in order to do the preliminary research for this project, which concluded in a doctor of ministry degree. Jan Skaggs and Constance Jordan-Haas lovingly read draft manuscripts and suggested critical changes.

Finally, to all of you who are working to build healthy ministries and good Christian communities, God bless you in your ministry team building!

Darien, Connecticut   GEORGE CLADIS
January 1999   *Noroton Presbyterian Church*

THE AUTHOR

GEORGE CLADIS is senior pastor and team leader at Noroton Presbyterian Church in Darien, Connecticut (in the greater New York City area). He earned his bachelor of arts degree (1976), magna cum laude in religious studies at the University of Colorado at Boulder, his master of divinity degree (1980) at Princeton Theological Seminary, Princeton, New Jersey, and his doctor of ministry degree (1986) from Austin Presbyterian Theological Seminary in Austin, Texas. Before joining Noroton Presbyterian Church, he served for eleven years as senior pastor of Covenant Presbyterian Church in Austin, Texas, where many of his ideas and concepts were put into practice. His primary research activities have centered around that team-based ministry in Austin, where he led a major, growing congregation. Church growth resulted in the addition of new staff who needed to be trained and assimilated into the life and culture of the congregation.

Cladis has also pastored churches in Colorado and west Texas, spoken at numerous retreats and conferences, worked as a consultant to congregations and their leadership boards, and contributed to various publications. While serving as a nonresident faculty member of Austin Presbyterian Theological Seminary, he was a supervisor in the Supervised Practice of Ministry program and also in the Teaching Church program: both programs were designed to help seminary students learn about the actual practice of ministry in a working congregation.

THE BIBLICAL CASE FOR TEAM-BASED MINISTRY

REFLECTING THE GOD WE SERVE

THE MOST EFFECTIVE churches today are the ones that are developing team-based leadership. This pattern will likely continue into the twenty-first century, both because Scripture emphasizes Spirit-led, Spirit-gifted, collaborative team fellowship and because today's culture is receptive to such leadership. In the church we are primarily concerned about building churches that reflect biblical standards. However, it also happens to be the case that certain leading voices in our culture are affirming models of participatory leadership. Part One discusses these two supports for team-based leadership.

The concepts and techniques for building effective church teams must first have a biblical and theological model that gives spiritual direction to team formation. Chapter One provides such a model and gives the theological grounding for everything that follows. It is the linchpin for the whole book.

In Chapter Two, I draw on the works of various innovators in organizational and business reform, including accounts of what makes certain businesses especially effective structurally. These works seek to revise the way organizations operate so they fit better with our emerging postmodern world. When I first started reading such books and essays, I realized there were certain key parallels between biblical concepts and the movement to reform organizational life. In fact, some of the language of organizational reform sounds remarkably *Christian.* For example, *Nuts! Southwest Airlines' Crazy Recipe for Business and Personal Success* (Freiberg and Freiberg, 1996) is not about God and religion, but the authors attribute much of Southwest Airlines' success to the fact that it treats customers *as sacred creations of God.* The authors write that Southwest views "customers as, to use Martin Buber's term, *sacred thous* who should be treated with dignity" (p. 316). I was amazed to read this kind of language in relation to a secular business enterprise. The Freibergs go on to say, "When the customer is a sacred thou, you scour the gate area for the lost teddy bear; you park his car when he's running late for a flight; you get out your credit card and pay for her ticket when she's lost her purse; and, yes, you even take him off the streets and give him a job" (p. 316).

Discovering biblical principles implied in various efforts to reform business and organizational life to fit a postmodern world, I asked myself, "What is the nature of this emerging postmodern culture and what aspects of it can help the church reform itself along biblical lines to be more effective? What can we learn from these reformers that fits our church environment?" My answers to these inquiries inform Chapter Two and the subsequent ideas for forming strong ministry teams for today's churches. In the seven key areas this book highlights, I illustrate how these cultural voices can help churches in making reforms toward team ministry. Just as Roman roads and the Pax Romana (Roman peace) contributed to the spread of Christianity, so certain (although not all) cultural factors today contribute toward the reorganization of churches along stronger biblical and theological lines to spread the Gospel more effectively.

In effect, then, this book is a conversation that carries ideas back and forth between Scripture and theology on the one hand and organizational reforms for a postmodern world on the other. This conversation results in the very practical steps recommended to form strong leadership teams in churches and Christian organizations, teams that will inspire the development of additional teams throughout their whole organizations.

LEARNING THE CIRCLE DANCE OF GOD

EFFECTIVE LEADERSHIP teams in the Church of Jesus Christ look to Scripture and Christian theology for their direction and shape. The culture of the church is thoroughly biblical, and who we leaders are and how we operate must be firmly grounded in Scripture. The biblical and theological model for team-based ministry that I present here is based on the triune nature of God. It is foundational for everything that follows.

Master Images

The postmodern world (defined more fully in Chapter Two) is an image-oriented world. People today spend several hours a day watching television compared to minutes reading a book or newspaper. Surfing the Internet is becoming a favorite pastime. The flow of images across our brains is training our minds to think more in images than in words. And these images have an effect on how we order the world around us and conceive of human community.

In different cultural contexts, different images of God have served as, in the language of Lawrence Hoffman (1988), *master images*. These controlling images have an effect on how we think about relationships and community, although we are often unconscious of it. Hoffman describes the master image in this way:

> A master image must be congruent with the cultural backdrop it expresses. . . . The "master image" of *Romeo and Juliet* (the picture you would expect to see on a *Playbill*, or the one you think of first as typifying the play's content) is the balcony scene; the reason it fits so

well, however, is not that there is something innately striking about balconies. Its success as a master image of the play is largely due to the fact that the physical distance between Juliet on the balcony and Romeo in the garden is symbolic of the play as a whole, whose theme, after all, is the unconquerable gulf between the two warring families of which Romeo and Juliet are members [p. 168].

A master image of the Book of Exodus is Moses and the Hebrew people marching down a path with a wall of water on either side of them. The master image for Judaism is the star of David and for Christianity it is the cross. Master images can have a profound, though sometimes subtle, effect on how we perceive reality.

In my search for meaningful ways to build and lead ministry teams in a postmodern world, I began to wonder what biblical master image could guide me as a church leader. What biblical picture could I hang on the wall of my mind to guide and shape my thoughts about leading church teams? If the images that surround us have such a dramatic effect on our faith and life, what image of God could I find in Scripture that would encourage healthy team ministry in the postmodern congregation?

A Dancing God

In the seventh century, John of Damascus, a Greek theologian, described the relationship of the persons of God (Trinity) as *perichoresis*. Perichoresis means literally "circle dance." *Choros* in ancient Greek referred to a round dance performed at banquets and festive occasions. The verb form, *choreuo*, meant to dance in a round dance. (These round dances often included singing, hence the English word *chorus*.) The prefix *peri* (Greek for *round about* or *all around*) emphasized the circularity of the holy dance envisioned by John. (For the Greek vocabulary, see *Greek-English Lexicon*, 1968; on perichoresis, see Guthrie, 1994, pp. 91–95; Volf, 1998, pp. 208–213.)

Based on the biblical descriptions of Father, Son, and Spirit, John depicted the three persons of the Trinity in a circle. A *perichoretic* image of the Trinity is that of the three persons of God in constant movement in a circle that implies intimacy, equality, unity yet distinction, and love.

Theologian Shirley Guthrie (1994) calls this image of God a "lovely picture" that portrays the persons of the Trinity in a kind of "choreography" (Greek *choros-graphy*), similar to a ballet. In this circle dance of God is a sense of joy, freedom, song, intimacy, and harmony. "The oneness of God is not the oneness of a distinct, self-contained individual; it is the unity of a *community* of persons who love each other and live together in harmony" (p. 92).

Guthrie goes on to describe the concept of God in perichoresis as significantly different from the more common Western medieval symbol of the Trinity as a triangle. Originally, the three sides of the triangle were meant to represent the three persons of God in a pure geometric symbol. Over time, however, the points of the triangle came to be commonly thought of as the persons of God, with the Father "on top." This view reinforced a hierarchical view of God and reality, represented in the hierarchies of both church and empire.

Letty Russell, in her book *Church in the Round* (1993), develops a theology and ecclesiology based on the *round table* of God, and she calls for "round table leadership" that reflects the circle fellowship of God. Distinctions between clergy and laity that have reinforced the centuries-old hierarchy need to be eliminated. Ordination should represent service rather than privilege and the power to dominate (pp. 63–67).

The perichoretic model of God calls into question the traditional hierarchies of power, control, and domination that have formed the basis for church leadership in the past. The medieval church both borrowed its leadership structures from the leadership structures of the empire and then modeled hierarchical structures on the image of the reign of God over all creation. Old Testament illustrations of king and kingdom further underscored the idea that hierarchical power was the divine model of leadership. The postmodern era, however, calls for new leadership structures and the New Testament provides better examples of leadership than empire leading and maintaining.

The perichoretic symbol of the Trinity is more helpful to the church living in a postmodern world. Although we, as the creatures of God, are not equal to God, the divine community of the Trinity provides a helpful image for human community that reflects the love and intimacy of the Godhead. Hierarchical distinctions in human community give way to a sense of the body of Christ, with each part equal and important (1 Cor. 12–14). The individual persons of the church are distinct parts yet are bound together in a common sharing and loving relationship.

The Trinity is one of the most often used descriptions of God in Christian worship around the world. We read about God the Father, Son, and Spirit in Scripture. We hear it in our creeds: "I believe in God, the Father Almighty . . . and in Jesus Christ, his only Son, our Lord . . . I believe in the Holy Spirit." From Matthew, chapter 28, Christians learn from the risen Lord to go into the world, "baptizing in the name of the Father, the Son and the Holy Spirit." And on any given Sunday, thousands of church services end with a benediction giving God's blessing to the people in the name of the Trinity. There is probably no more employed word image of God than that of Trinity.

The depiction of God as perichoretic Trinity is an excellent biblical and theological model for building meaningful ministry teams in the church of the twenty-first century.

The Icon of Andrei Rublev

During most summers of my childhood, my family traveled from the San Francisco Bay Area to Denver, Colorado, to be with our extended Greek American family. I fondly recall many outings and Greek Orthodox Church *fellowship suppers* during which we feasted on traditional Greek foods and then broke into a rousing circle dance. Men, women, and children all joined hands moving round and round in rhythm to the sounds of traditional Greek music.

When my wife, as my fiancée, came to California at Christmastime to meet my parents, we had a family supper of roasted lamb, lemon potatoes, and koriatiki salad, and then my father suggested we move into the living room for Christmas music. My wife imagined Bing Crosby singing traditional tunes. She wondered though why my parents were busy moving the furniture. I will never forget the expression on her face when, putting on Greek Christmas music, my parents led us in a circle dance to celebrate the Lord's birth.

In a circle, we can see each other. No one is left out. We are all interconnected. We hold each other up.

I once asked church innovators William Easum *(Sacred Cows Make Gourmet Burgers)* and Leonard Sweet (coeditor of the journal *Homiletics*) about worship targeted for unchurched people. How do we reach the younger generation today with the Gospel of Jesus Christ? They both suggested round tables.

"Round tables?" I said, puzzled.

"Yes," they replied, "and have the ushers be waiters, serving hot coffee."

Round tables. Immediately I thought of God in perichoresis. Round tables create a sense of community and wholeness. Have you ever tried to have a discussion with people sitting next to you on a long couch? Then why, in the church, do we still use so many long rectangular tables or pews? Sitting, standing, or dancing in the round, we feel together. A sense of community is immediately communicated.

Maybe that is why Andrei Rublev painted his famous icon of the Holy Trinity with the three persons of God seated at a round table (see Exhibit 1).

Exhibit 1. Rublev's Icon of the Holy Trinity.

Andrei Rublev (1360-c.1430). Icon of the Old Testatment Trinity, c.1410.
Tretyakov Gallery, Moscow, Russia.

Rublev, a fifteenth-century Russian Orthodox monk, painted the icon in memory of Saint Sergius, a Russian saint of the fourteenth century. Henri Nouwen (1987) has said, "I have never seen the house of love more beautifully expressed than in the icon of the Holy Trinity" (p. 20). The *house of love* he called it. And so it is. In building quality ministry teams, do we not also want to reflect God's house of love?

The Rublev icon portrays the Trinity in perichoresis. Orthodox theologians Ouspensky and Lossky (1982) believe this icon to be "the greatest of works" in portraying the Trinitarian teaching of the church.

> [The icon has] action, expressed in gestures, communion, expressed in the inclining of the heads and postures of the figures, and a silent, motionless peace. This inner life, uniting the three figures enclosed in the circle and communicating itself to its surroundings, reveals the whole inexhaustible depth of this image. It echoes, as it were, the words of Saint Dionysius the Areopagite, according to whose interpretation "circular movement signifies that God remains identical with Himself, that He envelops in synthesis the intermediate parts and the extremities, which are at the same time containers and contained, and that He recalls to Himself all that has gone forth from Him."
>
> . . . The Angels [the three persons of the Trinity] are grouped on the icon in the order of the Symbol of Faith, from left to right: I believe in God the Father, the Son and the Holy Spirit. . . . Unifying the three figures by their colouring, Rublev seems to point to the single nature of the Persons of the Holy Trinity, and also gives the whole icon a tranquil and lucid joyfulness [p. 202].

The three figures of the Trinity, sitting around the table, with the Eucharist present, appear to provide a place at the table for the faithful who behold the icon. This representation of the Trinity in joy, freedom, and equality implies an invitation to fellowship at the table.

An Invitation to the Dance

At a recent meeting of pastors from some of America's largest churches, I heard sung the same song I have heard many times.

"My church-affiliated school principal quit in a storm over school policy issues," complained a midwestern pastor. "He left the church for another in the city and took five hundred of our members with him."

"I'm in World War III with my music director," moaned a southern California minister. "I'm going to throw him out if he tries to mess with me any more."

"One of my associate pastors cornered me in an argument. I felt cold and sexually harassed," said a female pastor. "I think it was a power play; a way to intimidate me."

These comments reflect the tense relationships that seem to occur far too frequently in church leadership environments. Church members are often at first amazed that such things go on in the church office, but then they realize that the tensions at play in the church are not so different from the tensions that need to be managed in their own business offices. The image of God in perichoretic harmony grates against the reality of difficult work environments. We in the church should not be the last to realize the great need for reformation in work relationships, be they in the church or in secular contexts. We need to take a leadership role, working with those who seek to bring about better work environments and adding our important ingredient of the life-changing power of Jesus Christ. Why should the church, entrusted with the Gospel, be the last to introduce reforms to work environments?

Our leadership role must begin with an image to strive for. On the one hand it is both idyllic and absurd to think that our work groups and ministry teams could be like the Father, Son, and Spirit in perichoretic unity as described by Ouspensky and Lossky, in "a tranquil and lucid joyfulness." On the other hand, if we do *not* move toward an image, a goal, of spiritually meaningful and effective team ministry, our failure will surely result in relational breakdown, the result of human sin.

In reflecting on Rublev's icon, Henri Nouwen also considered the historical context out of which it grew:

> Saint Sergius, in whose honor and memory Rublev painted the Trinity icon, wanted to bring all of Russia together around the Name of God so that its people would conquer "the devouring hatred of the world by the contemplation of the Holy Trinity."
>
> Fear and hatred have become no less destructive since the fourteenth century, and Rublev's icon has become no less creative in calling us to the place of love, where fear and hatred no longer can destroy us.
>
> I pray that Rublev's icon will teach many how to live in the midst of a fearful, hateful, and violent world as they move always deeper into the house of love [pp. 26–27].

Can the perichoretic image of the Trinity teach us something about ministry teams in a postmodern world? Yes! From the model of God as perichoretic community, we can derive seven key attributes of church leadership teams that are both spiritually meaningful and practically effective for ministry in a postmodern world.

Church in the Round

These are the seven attributes that church leadership teams will strive for in a healthy ministry.

The Covenanting Team

Within the nature of God there is community. God the Father, Son, and Spirit are in relationship with one another and yet are one God. There is implicit in the love between Father, Son, and Spirit a sense of *covenant:* a living definition of community whose essence is love. Although they are not separate entities as human beings are, requiring contracts to define vows and obligations, they are nonetheless in relationship with one another. That relationship itself constitutes a form of living covenant, a character of relationship, the nature of which has been revealed to us in Scripture (at least in part). The unity of love and purpose within the Godhead resembles a covenant "written upon the heart" that is lived out perfectly in love.

In Scripture we also discover that God desires to expand the loving fellowship of the Trinity to include human beings. God did this historically by establishing covenants with us. In these covenants, God sought to establish a relationship to abolish the ancient enmity between God and humanity and create a new sense of community. These covenants historically defined the relationship between God and a human community (for example, Israel), established acceptable ways of acting and behaving in covenantal love, created a bond and affinity, and represented a sacred vow. Covenants between God and us forged the basis for the relationship upon which everything else was built.

Just as God covenanted with us, so we seek to covenant with one another as a basis for a good community. Although God's covenant with us is between creator and creatures and is therefore not between equals, our covenants with one another should seek to resemble the love of God—Father, Son, and Spirit—in holy fellowship. These covenants define how we will be with one another and what unites us.

Ministry teams are communities that covenant to be in fellowship together and live out the love of God. The members of these teams covenant with one another both to be in a relationship of God's love and to agree on their purposes and plans and the ways to move toward their fulfillment. The covenant, either written or verbal, describes and defines team members' relationship as a ministry team. The covenant describes how their love will be lived out both in their own team community and in the communities of the congregation and society. Ways and methods of doing ministry are defined and agreed upon. The covenant forms the basis for their community.

Ministry teams that covenant to be in community with one another and have a central purpose are a powerful unit of ministry. Their power comes not from themselves but from the Spirit, who acts to create their community, gives them a sharp vision for ministry, and binds them one to another. Although team covenants may specify what constitute good working relationships, the goal of the covenant is not to create tight boxes for conformity. Rather, the covenant gives order to passion and sets forth loving and honorable ways to be in relationship with one another. Paradoxically, the covenant gives freedom to explore and discover while at the same time it binds people in love to a common agreement that defines loving relationships.

The team covenant has several benefits for the ministry team. It first of all illustrates the relationship of team members, one to another, in positive, loving, and nurturing terms. The goal is to create a small community founded upon the love and grace of God in Jesus Christ. The covenant also can identify behaviors that work against the image of perichoretic love. Gossip, hierarchical thinking (triangulation), withholding pertinent information, and other dysfunctional activities are brought up and recognized as a threat to good community. A picture is painted in the covenant of persons committed both to serving God in mission and to working at their own sense of community, which can either enhance that mission or sabotage it. The covenant is a powerful tool for creating a setting of love that the team members hold each other accountable for upholding. To go against the covenant is not to go against the principal leader (for example, the pastor) but to sabotage the effort of the whole team.

The Visionary Team

God is sovereign and acts with intention. We experience life at times as cruel and arbitrary. The biblical witness, however, affirms that history is moving under God's sovereign direction toward a particular goal. We move from the Garden of Eden to the New Jerusalem for reasons God has established. As history unfolds, we experience the hand of God working to redeem and rebuild. Scripture reveals the activity of God as Father, Son, and Holy Spirit moving and acting in our midst with a clear purpose. We are being led. Whether it was through the wilderness of Sinai with Moses or into Samaria with Jesus, God has led and is leading us with purpose and design.

At the baptism of Jesus, God the Father spoke and the Spirit like a dove descended. The blessing of God was upon the Son for the purpose that he was commissioned to do. The fellowship of God—Father, Son, and Spirit—is wrapped up in loving purpose to redeem and restore.

The ministry teams whose members covenant to love one another and to exhibit God's community to the world must also have a clear sense of divine mission; it must be visionary. These teams seek to imitate God by creating meaningful communities that act with divine purpose and intent. Ministry teams are fueled by a mission God has given them to go and do. They act with purpose and design to fulfill God's will as best they can discern it.

Visionary teams are an effective means of accomplishing God's purposes because they are focused and goal oriented. They sense that their work has ultimate meaning, they sense that they are proceeding to do something highly significant, and they are clear about what each team member's role is in accomplishing the objective. Visionary teams are prayerful teams because they know that they can overcome the obstacles in their path only through the power of the Spirit who is guiding and directing them.

The Culture-Creating Team

The community of the Father, Son, and Spirit is a culture of love. The love of God, the divine purpose of God, the manner in which God has chosen to be revealed to us, the nature of God presented to us, all form a culture, a Kingdom, of God. This Kingdom of God has been especially revealed to us in the person of Jesus Christ. His life was an example to us of a life fully immersed in the culture of God.

Jesus taught us that the Kingdom of God is different from the world in which we live (Matt. 6:33); it is a healing presence (Matt. 9:35); its secrets are unveiled to us by Jesus (Matt. 13:11); it might not look like much but do not evaluate it as the world evaluates movements (Matt. 13:24,33); and it represents tremendous love (Luke 15). The church has been given remarkable authority to act in concert with God for the sake of the Kingdom (Matt. 16:19).

God calls the Church of Jesus Christ to exhibit the Kingdom of God to the world. We are to be culture creators. Jesus said, "Go therefore and make disciples of all nations, baptizing them in the name of the Father and of the Son and of the Holy Spirit, and teaching them to obey everything that I have commanded you. And remember, I am with you always, to the end of the age" (Matt. 28:19–20). We are sent out to preach and teach the Kingdom and make disciples, baptizing them into the reign of God. (It might be even more accurate to say we are enabled by God to be *counter*culture creators.)

The ministry team that covenants to be together in love and unity and to lead on the basis of a God-given vision then sets to work creating a culture of perichoretic love. The postmodern world is full of culture creators. Ministry teams endeavor to create the culture of the perichoretic fellowship of God. In so doing, they and thus their churches offer an alternative to the destructive and dysfunctional cultures around us. By reinforcing the things of God in Christian fellowship and service, ministry teams seek to bring to others the redemptive community of God.

By creating a culture of perichoretic love that is moving toward a God-given vision, teams reinforce the mission God has given the team and church to pursue. The culture supports the values of the Kingdom of God and is specific to the vision set before them. Creating such a culture keeps the team aware of its covenant and cause. A strong team culture keeps the team focused on what God calls it to do and be.

The team-created culture that is specific to the vision for the church's ministry becomes the basis for the congregation's culture as well. The leadership team immerses itself in a culture it then cultivates with the congregation. Culture creating is a very powerful way to influence teams and congregations with the values and narratives that support a vision. It becomes a nonverbal sermon that expresses what the team and church are all about.

When we build a strong team and church culture, we will attract those who resonate with the mission supported by that culture. Such a culture builds a strong force—a movement—for the purpose God has set before the church.

The Collaborative Team

There is no competition among the persons of God. Although *exactly* how the Trinity relates as Father, Son, and Spirit is enshrouded in mystery, Scripture describes God as these three persons yet one God. In God there is perfect harmony and community. Even though we experience the Father, Son, and Spirit in what seem to be different roles, they are nonetheless of one mind and substance. The idea that the Son would work against the ministry of the Spirit is entirely incongruous with the nature of God. That the Father would be jealous of the Son is absurd. There is, in the nature of God, what we might call perfect collaboration.

The ministry team whose members covenant together to give visionary leadership creates a church culture that models collaboration. Collaboration is not uniformity. Collaboration is coming to the table with spiritual gifts to be used in ministry. When the gifts are freely offered for ministry, God blesses and creates the spiritual synergy resulting from the team members' collaboration.

Collaboration works against competition. The collaborative team recognizes the unique gifts of its members and makes those members shine. They render one another's weaknesses irrelevant to the cause because they focus instead on each other's gifts and pool them to move toward the mission God has given the team. The collaborative team is able to reinforce the cultural value that each person is a child of God created in love for a purpose. Team members seek to model that value in their community by collaborating and valuing each other's contributions.

The Trusting Team

God exudes trust. It is the Lord's character to be trustworthy. The perfect community of the Trinity implies perfect trust. There is no sense that the Son betrays the Father or the Spirit lies and is deceitful. These things go against the character of God. Scripture instead reveals that God keeps promises, creates and holds to covenants, and establishes trust.

Broken trust destroys community and fellowship. The sin of disobedience in the garden (Gen. 3) was the result of the serpent's success in persuading the first human beings that God could not be trusted. Adam and Eve's distrust of God and willful disobedience resulted in enmity between humanity and God and enmity among human communities.

The ministry team whose members covenant together to give visionary leadership creates a church culture that models collaboration and trust. Ministry teams, filled with the Spirit of God, seek to mend broken community, and their members must therefore learn to trust one another and model trustworthiness. There is no more powerful way to break up relationships than to break trust. Merely the suspicion that a person cannot be trusted can result in severe fragmentation.

Yet what a powerful force for good and God's sacred mission is the team that builds trust! In a world that thrives on betrayal and deceit, a culture of trust created by a trusting team is a wonderful source of healing and ministry in the church and the world. The benefits of building a team such as this are immense.

The Empowering Team

God in perichoretic fellowship is constantly giving. Scripture is full of the giving of God for us and our salvation. It is the nature of God to pour out self, to extend grace, to give up life for us, that is, to be emptied that we might be full. Movement in the round is a surrendering of place while moving into a place given to us. We surrender, we empty, and then we receive.

Ministry team members in perichoretic fellowship covenant to work together, focus the church's vision, create a church culture that models collaboration and trust, take appropriate risks to innovate, and surrender their responsibility in order to empower others. Their responsibility is to give away responsibility. Their task is to empower others so that they may learn and grow and be all that God calls them to be. The person who seizes and hoards power robs other people of their God-given tasks and giftedness. Perichoretic leadership lifts up the responsibilities of others rather than taking responsibility away.

Empowering teams are very effective teams for the Kingdom of God because they spread out power and flatten hierarchies. These teams reinforce the concept that there is no such thing as a passive Christian; all of us are called to mission and ministry. Empowering teams build strong, enduring churches because the responsibility for the mission of the church is widely shared. Increased participation builds a strong church and is consistent with biblical images and with exhortations to be the body of Christ.

The Learning Team

According to the tenets of traditional, orthodox Christianity, we would not say that God is *learning*. Rather, God is all knowing. God is revealed to us, however, in several ways. For example, God is revealed in the natural order, by the Spirit in times of prayer, through the good fellowship and counsel of the church, in the reading and proclamation of the Word, and in the celebration of the sacraments. Ours, then, is a role of discovering and experiencing the revealed presence of God. As God is unfolded to us in many ways, we behold the glory of God, learn of the character of God, and seek to imitate the one in whose image we are made.

God is working to sanctify us in the Spirit. *Sanctification* is the doctrine that teaches us that we are being remade in the image of God. God is at work shaping and forming us into the people God originally intended us to be.

The ministry team that covenants together, articulates the church's vision, and creates a church culture that models collaboration and trust is also a team that is deepening its own sense of discipleship and learning. Ministry teams must be growing, learning teams. They are growing communities that are being shaped by the Spirit more and more in the image of God. These same teams experiment and take risks with what they have learned and experienced. Ministry teams are innovative, constantly seeking to apply their learning in practical ways. Their learning, both spiritual and practical, becomes a narrative of growth that can help other teams and churches grow spiritually and become more effective communities of ministry.

The vibrant twenty-first century church is well led when it has ministry teams that reflect the perichoretic fellowship and love of God. These teams are covenanting, visionary, culture creating, collaborative, trusting, empowering, and learning. These team characteristics also fit well with the emerging postmodern world.

2

BUILDING ON A RECEPTIVE CULTURAL ENVIRONMENT

THERE ARE MANY reasons why team-based ministry is the most theologically and culturally appropriate method for church leadership today. Chapter One introduced the theological model that supports team-based ministry. This chapter shows how our current cultural context forms a receptive environment for these biblically based church teams.

Cultural observers and leaders in many fields of study acknowledge that we have passed from the *modern* era into a new cultural age, which they are calling the *postmodern* era. Certain characteristics of this postmodern world support a team-based ministry in two ways. First, they suggest new models for leadership that strike me as more biblically and theologically sound than the leadership models traditionally used in congregations. Through these models, the postmodern culture actually encourages good reforms in the church. Second, because the people whom we seek to reach with the Gospel are, like most people, heavily influenced by the social culture, team-based ministry fits well with their ideas and their experiences.

Some readers will respond that I am suggesting the church accommodate itself to culture. On the one hand there are certain things about postmodern culture that Christians find appalling. Certainly the church must never simply march to the beat of the cultural drummer. We are called to live a Kingdom that is in this world but not of it. On the other hand, just as a missionary to a foreign land seeks to learn the local customs, dialects, foods, and traditions—that is, its *culture*—in order to evangelize, so we can draw out those things in culture that are supportive of our message and use those in our ministry. The cultural relevance of a biblically sound team-based ministry actually can increase its effectiveness in reaching out to postmodern people.

What then is postmodern culture and what characterizes it?

A Paradigm Shift

Scholars in many different fields of study agree that Western society is moving through a major cultural change from modernism to postmodernism (see, for example, Anderson, 1995b). The term *postmodernism,* naming the epoch just dawning in terms of its not being the previous epoch, suggests the lack of a single set definition for this new era. Postmodern culture is a complex set of societal variables that reflect a recent shift in the way people in Western society think, and this paradigm change is having dramatic effects on the life of the church as an organization. It turns our whole way of thinking about and conceiving of human communities and systems upside down. Postmodernism, Walter Truett Anderson (1995a) writes, "is a major transition in human history, a time of rebuilding all the foundations of civilization, and the world is going to be occupied with it for a long time to come" (pp. 7–8).

Modernism was a period obsessed with organizing, standardizing, and categorizing reality into one system of understanding. On the one hand, it enabled people to develop better tools of agriculture and transportation. Our ability to combat disease increased, and living conditions were dramatically improved. On the other hand, modernism represented an ethos of competition and hierarchy that tended to force people into roles that took away their identity as children of God and made them instead cogs in a vast, cosmic machine.

Postmodernism has emerged as a radically different view of reality that has, in part, reacted against the cold nature of modernism. The postmodern world hungers for meaning and spirituality that the modern world tended to strip away. Individuals and their unique gifts are valued equally, and collaboration between networks or communities of people are emphasized, as opposed to large, colorless, hierarchical bureaucracies. The postmodern world is not entirely attractive to Christians. It is accompanied by a sense of relativism produced by a pluralistic world that results in a collage of behaviors and values that Christians tend to find appalling.

However, when we look more closely at postmodern culture, we can also surface specific characteristics that contain wonderful new opportunities for the Church of Jesus Christ to be reformed and renewed along biblical lines.

The following nine key characteristics of postmodern culture, radical changes that have taken place in the last couple of decades, tell us where churches need to change to minister more effectively to this new culture. All nine are related to the seven attributes of a leadership team outlined in Chapter One and developed in the chapters in Part Two. Some characteristics relate closely to a specific attribute, some relate more generally to several attributes. Together, they create a sense of the cultural milieu that actually contributes to the effectiveness of church-based ministry teams.

NINE POSTMODERN CHARACTERISTICS

Creation is an organism rather than a machine.

Hierarchical structures are reduced.

Authority is based on trust.

Effective leadership is visionary.

Life and work are spiritually rooted.

Structures are smaller; networks are bigger.

Innovation is rewarded.

Work follows gifts, and gifts are used collaboratively.

Mainline church domination has ended.

An examination of these characteristics in more depth will create a cultural backdrop for the rest of the book.

Creation Is an Organism Rather Than a Machine

In the modern world the objective was to know all the variables and control them. Nature was to be analyzed, explained, measured, and manipulated to the point that it could be predicted. "A vast and complex machine [nature] had been entrusted to our care," writes Margaret Wheatley (1992, p. 29). It was our job to figure out how it worked. With that information, we could control nature to our advantage.

Organizations that controlled their human variables could then predict the outcome, whether it be greater production of widgets or an efficiently operated Boy Scout Jamboree. Vast personnel processes and systems were developed to define jobs, specify behaviors, identify tasks clearly and distinctly, and then recruit people to fulfill tightly cast roles. By controlling all of the human *parts,* it was thought, the future of the organization could be predicted. A pyramidal and hierarchical structure processing orders from above kept each part in its place to perform its function accordingly. This structure was considered the model for a strong organization. "A world based on machine images is a world filled with boundaries," observes Wheatley. "In a machine, every piece knows its place. . . . We've created roles and accountabilities, drawing lines of authority and limits to responsibilities" (p. 28).

Nature, however, is perceived differently in the postmodern world. Instead of viewing the universe as a grand machine (and one to be imitated in our workplaces), the postmodernist sees creation as more like a living organism. The emphasis today is not so much on controlling all the variables of nature—an impossible task—but instead on learning about it, discovering the interaction of its parts, and exploring its many and diverse relationships.

Hierarchical Structures Are Reduced

Corporate reengineering experts of the late 1980s and 1990s Michael Hammer and James Champy (1993) sounded the alarm: the traditional ways of doing business for organizations today "simply don't work anymore. Suddenly, the world is a different place" (p. 17). Margaret Wheatley concurred, the old way of doing organizational business simply "does not work" (p. 25). And one of those things now rendered obsolete in organizational life, according to Hammer and Champy, is the old "pyramidal organizational structure." It too simply does not work in our new culture.

Effective work groups in the postmodern world do not emphasize hierarchy. It is a structure that does not motivate people to give their best. Instead, the interchange of ideas among everyone involved in an enterprise is valued and considered important. A premium is put on including people in decision making rather than excluding them. Hierarchical structures tended to stifle innovation. Only the creativity of the few *on top* was felt throughout an organization. *Flatter* structures draw out the innovation of all work group members not just of a few. Furthermore, those working in flatter settings feel more a part of a team accomplishing an objective that has meaning and not simply like people doing a job.

Max De Pree is chairman emeritus of Herman Miller, Inc., and author of several books on leadership, marketed primarily to secular business and organizational leaders. What is one of the ingredients of his formula for successful leadership? Servanthood. "The best description of this kind of leadership," writes De Pree (1992) to his secular readership, "is found in the book of Luke: 'The greatest among you should be like the youngest, and the one who rules, like the one who serves'" (p. 10). Postmodern writers are even using Scripture to back their points!

Old-style church organizations are having a difficult time adjusting to the postmodern world. People no longer respond well to orders from superiors. When it comes time for difficult decisions to be made, people are finding it harder to hear, "the bishop has decided," "the pastor says," or, "the Presbytery says you have to do it this way," when they themselves have not been thoroughly involved in the decision-making process. If the bishop is distant from the people of a congregation or the presbytery a vague consortium of strangers, their decisions that affect the life of the local congregation are likely to be resented. People in the postmodern world do not experience resentment passively. They leave. Consequently, churches that do not shift the way they operate in the postmodern world tend to have a difficult time surviving.

Ministry teams that are open, available, flexible, responsive, and representative of the people they lead will do better in the postmodern world than will leaders at the top of an old-style hierarchical pyramid. Postmodernism requires organizations to turn the pyramid upside down so that leaders who were above are now below. And instead of giving orders from above, they give support to the wider constituency from below.

Authority Is Based on Trust

In the modern world, credentials and titles meant more than they do in the postmodern world. Although educational and professional accomplishments are still important and required for many careers—even positions in churches—they carry less authority with the average church member. Years of education may not produce a good pastor. Other gifts and skills are also needed that cannot be learned in a seminary environment.

Postmodern people recognize the right of others to lead them more on the basis of trust and relational credit than of titles and credentials. The clerical vestment, a symbol of the ordained office and the authority granted by the church to a pastor to preach and administer the sacraments, is not nearly as meaningful today as it was years ago. The postmodern world wants to know the heart of its leadership. Words like *authentic* and *genuine* are being used to describe effective and able leaders. The most important question for those who would follow a leader is no longer, Does she have the educational and professional requirements to fill this position? but rather, Is she trustworthy and will she listen to my concerns? Jackson Carroll (1991), for example, researching the recent shift in the nature of pastoral authority in the church, reports that "clergy found that personal authority, based on effective pastoral care, became more important for their legitimacy than authority of office" (p. 70).

The church in the postmodern world has a wonderful opportunity to rediscover the importance of leading from the heart and from strongly held convictions. Leading on the basis of trust builds a strong community in which relationships are founded upon mutual concerns. The typical church member is more likely to *own* a sense of ministry and mission when led by those whom he trusts rather than by those who lead using guilt and command. For example, the apostle Paul wrote to the Thessalonians beautiful words that reflect postmodern leadership values: "But we [apostles of Christ] were gentle among you, like a nurse tenderly caring for her own children. So deeply do we care for you that we are determined to share with you not only the gospel of God but also our own selves, because you have become very dear to us" (1 Thess. 2:7–8).

Ministry teams, to be effective in the postmodern world, must create trust among their members and trust with those whom they serve. Authority is given to them on the basis of the relational history of the team and the church members and their mutual ownership of a church vision, a vision team members articulate as authentic individuals engaged in ministry from the heart and soul. Carroll discovered that "a willingness to make one's self vulnerable, to show empathy, to express care and compassion, to tell the truth, to be just, to seek the good of the individual or that of the community—such qualities create a kind of 'mystical geography' that bonds the pastor and parishioner in a common relational turf" (p. 197). These characteristics, says Carroll, build strong bonds of trust between people.

Effective Leadership Is Visionary

In the modern world, management meant ensuring that employees had clear job descriptions and were doing the work prescribed by managers. An unproductive worker was one not fulfilling her job description. The manager would walk the employee through several clearly laid out steps to remind her of her terms of service spelled out in the job description. Various levels of threat and probation were used to make sure that the employee either learned to do the job as outlined or faced termination. Managing people, then, was managing units of production matched with position descriptions. The good manager was the one who could keep his units in line, producing goods or services. We "created trouble for ourselves in organizations by confusing control with order," says Wheatley. "This is no surprise, given that for most of its written history, management has been defined in terms of its control functions" (p. 22).

In the postmodern world, people are less likely to be motivated by this kind of management. Workers today demand more contractual arrangements, in which they agree to give their labor in exchange for money and also *meaning*. Money is not enough. People want their work to be worthwhile. Filling a job description is not enough. The job description itself needs to be founded on something significant so it can motivate people from the heart.

Postmodern managers must learn to cast a vision for their workers to follow. The vision gives a context for the labor or service that goes beyond the mere doing of it. The vision inspires workers, envisioning a future that they want to see come about. It becomes for them a sacred mission, a cause, that motivates them beyond money or prestige. "Helping people believe in the importance of their work is essential," writes Rosabeth Moss Kanter (1997), professor of management at Harvard Business School. This is true "especially when other forms of certainty and security have disappeared. Good leaders can inspire others with the power and excitement of their vision and give people a sense of purpose and pride in their work. Pride is often a better source of motivation than the traditional corporate career ladder and the promotion-based reward system" (p. 145).

Biblical leaders were such visionary leaders. Given a call by God, they motivated people on the basis of something beyond them all that had ultimate meaning. With such a vision, Nehemiah united the Israelites to build a wall around the city of Jerusalem. They knew they had a role in building something for godly purposes.

The postmodern world should remind church leaders and ministry teams that church membership is not a passive thing but a signing up for a mission and ministry that has ultimate significance. The need of postmodern people to find meaning and significance in what they do fits well the biblical mandate to make *disciples* rather than passive pew sitters.

Life and Work Are Spiritually Rooted

In the modern world, life was something you lived when work was over. From eight to five you did your job. When the five o'clock whistle blew, you could do what you enjoyed. Work was a means to an end: the living of your life as you chose rather than as you were ordered to do. U.S. workers agreed to mindless, routine production line labor in exchange for a paycheck that allowed them to live above a bare sustenance level and to develop hobbies and recreation in their "off" time.

Postmodern people do not tolerate such a sharp delineation between mundane activity and meaningful even *sacred* activity. Spiritual concerns mark postmodern culture. People today are looking for links to the divine in what they do.

The trend toward seeking a spiritual foundation for all of life, *including* work, can be found in the popularity of certain recent business publications. Stephen Covey's huge success, *The Seven Habits of Highly Effective People* (1990), emphasized the linkage between spiritual values and all activities of an individual's life. Business and organizational thinkers Lee Bolman, Terrence Deal, and Alan Briskin also evidence the need for postmodern people to find spiritual meaning in their lives, including their working relationships. These writers argue that society today hungers not only for work that is participatory but also spiritually satisfying. As Bolman and Deal say in *Leading with Soul: An Uncommon Journey of Spirit* (1995), "In the work place, all of us need a language of moral discourse that permits discussions of ethical and spiritual issues, connecting them to images of leadership" (pp. 2–3). Business leadership, then, is not just about making money. It is about leading with soul or connecting work with deeper spiritual issues. Writing out of a business background and to a primarily managerial crowd, Bolman and Deal sound remarkably *religious:* "What has escaped us is a deep understanding of the spirit, purpose, and meaning of human experience" (p. 8). Briskin writes out of a similar perspective in *The Stirring of Soul in the Workplace* (1996). He urges leaders to embark on an odyssey of self-discovery that goes "deeper, down into a place in which past and future blur, where what we strive for and what drives us can be glimpsed" (p. 11). These writers reveal the deep longings of organizational thinkers for something more than flip charts and bar graphs: the spiritual grounding of the workplace.

The church faces a wonderful opportunity today to give spiritual meaning to the workplace: the church office as well as the business office. Postmodern hunger for things spiritual opens doors to Christian evangelism. It reminds me of the opportunities people's spiritual needs gave to the church in the first century A.D. Ministry teams and other work groups that view their work together in deeply spiritual terms, reflecting the love and community of the Trinity, for example, fit well into the postmodern world.

Structures Are Smaller; Networks Are Bigger

Postmodern society distrusts large bureaucracies. The 1980s and 1990s reveal a dismantling of these large management structures. Peter Drucker (1989, pp. 10–17) has called the modern age a time of salvation of people through huge state systems. Examples of such systems are Soviet communism, Third Reich fascism in Germany, and even the Great Society proposed by Lyndon Johnson. People today, however, find such systems and structures horribly inefficient and inhumane. Their foundational concepts stemmed from that modernist notion of the universe as a machine. One did one's duty as a cog in the machine for the sake of the machine's (society's) success. The postmodern understanding of our universe as more mysterious organism than quantified, measurable machine lends itself to a view of organizations as more networks of relationships than cumbersome multilayered structures. Today's tendency, then, is to make organizations smaller and leaner while extending their influence through an ever growing network of relationships.

Margaret Wheatley described the change from the Newtonian (modern) to the quantum (postmodern) world as producing considerable stress and change in the area of managing people and a corresponding need for new leadership skills. These skills have "taken on a relational slant. Leaders are being encouraged to include stakeholders, to evoke followership, to empower others. . . . We cannot hope to influence any situation without respect for the complex network of people who contribute to our organizations" (pp. 144–145). Before this new era, when we focused more on tasks than on relationships, these people were an "annoying inconvenience" (Wheatley, p. 144); now, they are those to whom leaders are "in debt" (De Pree, 1989, p. 11).

The postmodern distrust of bureaucracies and favoring of broad networks of relationships is wreaking havoc in traditional church denominations. The large, centralized denominational offices and structures are now archaic, and people have lost confidence in them. The change to smaller, leaner organizational structures is difficult and painful. But once again, I suggest there is a wonderful opportunity here for those of us in church leadership to be reminded that we are called to make disciples and not huge structures (see, for example, Mark 13:1–2). Relational ministry best sums up the ministry of Jesus. God did not send a committee or an organization to die on the cross for us. God sent the Son who loves us, teaches us, rebukes us, redeems us, and empowers us—all very relational dynamics! Ministry teams that are relational and network forming rather than bureaucratic have wonderful opportunities to grow and thrive in the postmodern world.

Innovation Is Rewarded

The postmodern world differs from the modern in that it values failure. One of the worst things you could be in the modern world was a failure. It meant you could not follow orders. Innovation and creativity were the responsibility of those "above," and you did not dare risk failure by trying something new. You did your job right—the way it was prescribed by your superior—even if you knew it could be done better another way.

The trend today is to recognize that those doing a job often have a good feel for how it can be done better. General Motors, for example, finally started to listen to the workers on the production line and discovered there were better, more efficient ways to make cars. There is implied in such listening the placing of a higher value on the individuals on the production line and their opinions. People who are drawn into the design phase of that which they produce have a higher sense of ownership of the product's ability to meet a specific need. Work for them becomes more meaningful and participatory.

Failure today is considered part of the learning curve we must travel to master new skills and techniques. No longer thinking of the universe as essentially a known quantity requiring us just to fill in the details of how it works, the postmodern individual sees the universe as still quite mysterious, requiring us to actively explore it. Exploration and discovery imply risk. Risk can result in failure. But the learning derived from that failure is more highly valued today than in the past because it is understood to be a necessary step toward successful innovation. "Failure is, simply, a shortfall, evidence of the gap between vision and current reality," writes Peter Senge (1990). "Failure is an opportunity for learning—about inaccurate pictures of current reality, about strategies that didn't work as expected, about the clarity of the vision. Failures are not about our unworthiness or powerlessness" (p. 154).

Ministry teams that risk, fail, learn, and grow are more likely to innovate—to draw accurate pictures of reality—and find meaningful ways to communicate the Gospel than are the teams that are fixed in rigid patterns. The postmodern characteristic of risk and discovery fits well the biblical mandate to venture out into new lands with the Gospel. Moreover, once we view the entire world (not just "foreign" places) as our missionary field, we will also assume that the culture, customs, language or dialect, and diet of our own places well as of new places must be learned in order to communicate effectively the Gospel of Jesus Christ.

Work Follows Gifts, and Gifts Are Used Collaboratively

The modern era emphasized tasks more than gifts. The important thing was whether a particular task was done and not so much whether a person was especially well equipped to do the task. A church might hire, for example, an associate pastor to do youth ministry without looking very deeply into that person's gifts for youth ministry. Although certain task credentials and experience might be required for a position, neither credentials nor experience alone will indicate whether or not a candidate actually has the passion or the gifts to do the job well. In the modern world, it even seemed odd to suggest that individuals *enjoy* their work. Work was not necessarily done for enjoyment. Rather, as suggested earlier, work was something that had to be done as a means to an end: the enjoyment of life came *after work*.

The postmodern world values gifts and passion as necessary for the successful accomplishment of tasks. Important questions that probe whether or not a potential employee has the passion and the gifts as well as the skills necessary to perform a task are part of the interview process. In work teams, people collaborate by pooling their resources and gifts to move toward a common goal. When people view the universe as a highly sensitive network of relationships rather than as a machine, they develop relationships to collaborate on various projects. Many today find a career niche in connecting people so they can combine their gifts to accomplish specific endeavors.

Collaboration implies reciprocal agreement. Group needs are met mutually by group members. Each exchanges his or her labor for a meaningful outcome that all participate in. "Fostering collaboration begins with creating and sustaining cooperative goals," say James Kouzes and Barry Posner (1995). "The best incentive for others to help you is knowing that you'll reciprocate, helping them in return. Help begets help just as trust begets trust" (p. 169). There is a depth of commitment created in collaborative teams that other group work models do not come close to creating.

The postmodern emphasis on gift-based work can be viewed in the light of Paul's description of the church as the body of Christ. Each member of the body has a unique role to play and is gifted by God to do it. We are interconnected in a network of relationships with Christ as the head. The postmodern trend toward relational networks can remind the church of the importance of each child of God and his or her gifts for ministry.

Mainline Church Domination Has Ended

Jackson Carroll, reflecting on the different way in which traditional churches are viewed today, finds that "what once seemed to be citadels of order, security, and timelessness—and thus a firm foundation for the authority of clergy who lead them—have, for many people, lost their aura of invincibility and absoluteness" (p. 34). Christendom is over in America. The surprising thing is that it seemed to happen so quickly! Earlier in my lifetime, a person was most likely to attend the kind of church in which he was raised. A Lutheran would attend the neighborhood Lutheran Church, and a Presbyterian would attend the Presbyterian Church. The independent church was the little clapboard church on the edge of town. No one of prestige in the community attended the independent church.

In a relatively short amount of time the religious scene has changed dramatically. Those once *invincible* orders of the mainline churches are in serious decline, and some observers question whether they will survive the next century. My own denomination—Presbyterian Church (U.S.A.)—has lost tens of thousands of members every year for more than twenty consecutive years. And it is not unique. Most of the traditional mainline Protestant denominations, so instrumental in forging the religious heritage of the United States, are experiencing huge losses.

Where is everyone going? One result of the increasingly pluralist nature of U.S. society has been the growth of religions from the Far East. And many people do not go to church at all. Nevertheless, a surprising large number of Americans still attend Christian churches weekly. More and more, however, they are attending large, independent churches or churches grouped together only in loose confederacies. University of Southern California professor of religion Donald Miller (1997) calls several of these growing, expanding Christian movements *new paradigm churches*. New paradigm churches, according to Miller's research, have "discarded many of the attributes of establishment religion." They have "appropriated contemporary cultural forms" and created "a new genre of worship music; they are restructuring the organizational character of institutional religion; and they are democratizing access to the sacred by radicalizing the Protestant principle of the priesthood of all believers" (p. 1). Furthermore, it is becoming more and more common for people who are mainline professionals in their jobs to attend these sprawling independent new paradigm churches.

The postmodern world is dismantling old-style institutions. Recall the words of Michael Hammer and James Champy and of Margaret Wheatley, the old way of doing organizational business simply "does not work." So many things associated with the strength of the former era have suddenly been rendered irrelevant. The order, styles, music, vestments, liturgies, structures, many of the symbols, and often the buildings themselves of traditional churches do not carry the meaning they once did. Suddenly, these churches have been found lacking in the fundamental activity of a religious community: mediating the sacred. I was shaken when I read Don Miller's indictment: "I argue that not only are new paradigm churches doing a better job of responding to the needs of their clientele than are many mainline churches, but—more important—they are successfully mediating the sacred, bringing God to people and conveying the self-transcending and life-changing core of all true religion" (p. 3).

Churches need to change to be effective in the twenty-first century. Traditional methods of doing ministry, in most cases, simply do not communicate across the chasm that has opened between the modern world in which traditional churches thrived and the postmodern world in which leaders and organizations are required to do something entirely new. Although this causes much stress and strain for the traditional churches, the good news is that in many areas the changes required work to reform the church to a more biblical model. And one of those areas is leadership, where we must attend to the higher value placed today on participatory, collaborative, team leadership.

Postmodern Opportunities

Some phenomena associated with postmodernism are not friendly to the church or its convictions. However, the nine characteristics I have described here demonstrate that many postmodern views can actually aid the church. They offer essential opportunities for all church leaders to recover effective and satisfying ways of doing ministry that go hand-in-hand with their biblical and theological beliefs.

PART TWO

THE DANCE OF LEADERSHIP

BUILDING GRACEFUL
MINISTRY TEAMS

THE PERICHORETIC nature of God as Trinity gives us seven key attributes of ministry teams that reflect the image and community of God. The ministry teams most effective for ministry in the twenty-first century will be teams that are covenanting, visionary, culture creating, collaborative, trusting, empowering, and learning. These attributes not only make theological sense, as discussed in Chapter One, but also fit well with the trends of a postmodern world, as outlined in Chapter Two. Some church leaders today, in fact, believe that our current cultural climate resembles that of the Roman Empire in the first century A.D.: the cradle of the early church. Reforming the church around these seven attributes, then, offers the church an opportunity to return to strong biblical themes and models of ministry.

The following seven chapters look at some practical ways to form a strong church leadership team around these seven attributes. The members of a principal leadership team will often be staff, that is, they will be paid. Other ministry teams may be made up of staff and volunteers or be all volunteers. Most of the suggestions made in this book apply equally to staff and to volunteer teams.

Each chapter, focusing on a single attribute, is built on a common outline. I discuss the attribute in question biblically and theologically, relating it to the model of God in perichoresis. I then look at how some contemporary organizational and business leaders are dealing with related cultural trends. My intent is to discuss each attribute in the theological context and in the cultural context. Each chapter also looks at actual examples of how other churches are incorporating the attribute into their church cultures. Finally, each chapter presents the practical ways the attribute can contribute to building an effective leadership team. In addition, Chapter Three opens with a description of a common leadership conflict in the fictitious, but true-to-life, First Church of Appleton. As the chapters proceed, they show how this typical congregation could use the steps presented to overcome leadership conflicts and build an effective leadership team and then to expand the team model throughout the church.

3

THE COVENANTING TEAM

FIRST CHURCH IS a 125-year-old traditional congregation located in Appleton, a midsized city in a well-known apple-growing part of its state. Although the city has grown and diversified with high technology and other light industries, Appleton continues to be widely known for its exceptional apple products. The First Church senior pastor is a well-known community leader who preaches excellent sermons. The church has grown in recent years to an average worshiping attendance of one thousand.

The senior pastor, the associate pastor for pastoral care, the associate pastor for youth ministry, the director of children's ministry, the director of music, and the business manager make up the full-time staff. Each represents various areas of ministry. For example, the pastor for pastoral care meets often with the hospital visitors, those who minister to the homebound, and lay counselors. At one time, each staff member felt primarily accountable to the lay leaders in his or her area of ministry. Staff salaries were even budgeted within the ministry area budgets. The director of music, for example, was paid out of the music budget rather than a comprehensive personnel budget. Staff offices were located near their ministry areas: the pastor for youth ministry worked in the youth wing, the music director's office was next to the choral rehearsing rooms, and so forth.

First Church, then, had various *tents* of ministry set up within one large congregation. Staff tended to minister to their own, developing lines of accountability to relationships among their own ministry constituents. Staff meetings, led by the senior pastor, were held every other week, lasted one hour, and focused on calendar coordination, making sure there was no overlap of facility use and that there was some order and logic to the scheduling of special events. The annual meeting for the preparation of the budget was a tug-of-war competition for resources to fund the various ministry areas.

The staff relationships at First Church grew strained as each member imagined others encroaching on his or her areas of ministry. One year, the music ministry received a larger portion of the budget increase, which infuriated youth leaders. The youth pastor along with other key youth leaders spread the word among those concerned about youth ministry in the congregation that the youth ministry did not get its fair share. Pressure was put on the board of elders to remedy the situation. Some parents, angry after hearing gossip that First Church no longer valued the youths of the congregation, threatened to change churches.

The music director thought the youth pastor was spreading erroneous information. He felt that both his program and his ministry were threatened by the perception that "youths were being sacrificed for a Christmas cantata." Some parents in the sanctuary choir quit the choir in protest. Other choir members and the elders on the music committee rallied support among their friends to defend the music program.

The board of elders met to discuss the growing dissatisfaction among youths' parents, choir members, and congregational leaders. Some at the meeting suggested delaying a planned playground renovation and adding those funds to the youth ministry, in an amount equal to the increase the music ministry received. The elders responsible for the children's ministry went ballistic. They had waited patiently for that playground renovation. "Parents of young children will be furious," they argued. In the end the elders voted to reduce the amount given to the music ministry so that the music ministry and the youth ministry would each receive the same amount. The result was hurt feelings all around, resentment, and further fragmentation among both the staff and their loyal constituents. The various tents of ministry seemed farther apart than before, and the congregation more divided along camp lines.

Ours Is a Covenanting God

What can we learn from God in perichoretic fellowship that can help us mitigate such damaging fractures as those experienced by First Church of Appleton and create healthy, covenanting ministry teams?

God's House of Love

God in perichoresis portrays to us the unity of God in three persons. There is a flow of affection, love, and unity among the three persons of the one God. Competition is alien within God. There is no sense in Scripture that the Son is resentful of the Spirit's ministry or that the Father interferes with the redemptive work of the Son. "If a house is divided against itself, that house will not be able to stand," Jesus said (Mark 3:25).

Recall that Henri Nouwen described Rublev's icon of the perichoretic fellowship of the Trinity as a house of love. The house of love, which is the self of God, models for us the peace, unity, and congruity we seek to move toward within our ministry teams. Another telling metaphor we might use comes from music. Just as a fine orchestra combines its many instruments to create a singular piece, so the persons of God are united in a symphony of love.

> God is One, unique and holy,
> Endless dance of love and light;
> Only source of mind and body,
> Star cloud, atom, day and night:
> Everything that is or could be
> Tells God's anguish and delight.
>
> —Brian Wren

God Extends the House of Love

We see God presented to us as a united fellowship of love; this fellowship then acts to extend the divine House of Love to encompass a creation broken by sin. Scripture reveals to us a God who establishes covenants with us as a way of uniting *us* in fellowship with God. These covenants initiated by God are formed out of the depths of God's love, grace, and forbearance. The biblical covenant typically involved the establishment of a relationship that specified certain behaviors and responsibilities. God chose to act redemptively toward the people in a community and to be their God. Their response to God's grace—a grace exemplified in the making of a covenant with them—was to serve the Lord and one another as laid out in the terms of the covenant.

God's covenants with Israel and other communities differ importantly from covenants between people (covenants between merchants or between equal nations, for example). God's covenants with us are between unequal parties; between a sovereign and servant. Take as an example the Mosaic covenant established at Mount Sinai, which created Israel as a nation with Yahweh as its God. As Old Testament scholar Bernard Word Anderson (1986) tells us, "the Mosaic covenant was in no sense a parity contract in which both parties were equal and mutually dependent. It was a relationship between unequals, between God and human beings; and the holiness and majesty of God are portrayed in the account of the awesome thunder and lightning before which the people stood back in fear. The covenant was *given* by God; the relationship was conferred upon the people by their Sovereign" (p. 101; emphasis added).

The covenant of God with Israel defined a gracious relationship initiated by a sovereign lord. Israel, however, was not merely a passive subject. The covenant embodied a vow between God and God's people. As Anderson explains, "Israel was bound to Yahweh, their Liberator, who had performed 'mighty acts' on their behalf. Therefore Israel's pledge of obedience, as expressed in the covenant ceremony ('All the words that Yahweh has spoken we will do'), was predicated on gratitude for Yahweh's marvelous goodness, in response to Yahweh's gracious initiative. Israel, in short, was beholden to Yahweh. Salvation was the basis for obligation" (p. 101).

Israel responded to God's gracious acts of deliverance in the Old Testament with worship. Exodus, chapters 19 and 24, preserves early examples of Israel's covenant renewal ceremony. Israel reappropriated both the terms and the love of the original Mosaic covenant through these worshipful experiences.

Covenants That Create Houses of Love

God is a house of love who acts to extend the fellowship of love to all creation. We can find in God's nature a model for forming human communities that will reflect God's house of love. This is, of course, a very difficult task. Human communities have struggled from the beginning of history to find ways to get along. From ancient times, one form of mutual cooperation or, at least tolerance, has been the treaty. Covenants and treaties are quite similar in their intent: they intend to bind two or more parties together with mutual responsibilities and commitments. Solomon, for example, made a treaty with Hiram, the king of Tyre, to supply timber to build the temple (1 Kings, 5). The Hebrew phrase for *treaty making* here is literally "to cut a covenant."

The Christian marriage service is a kind of covenant making that imitates God's covenants with us, except that it is between equal parties. Instead of being a covenant between a sovereign and servant, it is a covenant between a man and woman in equal partnership, called to be made one by the Spirit. Marrying is literally forming a new house of love. Like biblical covenants, the marriage service sets forth the terms of the agreement. Marriage involves duty, service, love, patience, tenderness, forgiveness, grace, forbearance, and obligation. The covenant vow defines the relationship and also what covenant love is like. It is remarkable to me how clearly and succinctly the terms of the covenant can be stated in this brief vow: "*N.*, do you acknowledge this Woman/Man to be your wedded wife/husband, and do you promise and covenant, before God and these witnesses, to be her/his loving and faithful husband/wife, in plenty and in want, in joy and in sorrow, in sickness and in health, as long as you both shall live?" (United Presbyterian Church, 1946, p. 190).

Team Houses of Love

Team covenants, too, are forged between equal partners. Each person is respected as a child of God who is gifted for service in the church. The team leader is not conceived of as a sovereign over subjects but as an equal child of God whose function is to lead through service and the building of covenantal ministry teams. The leader's task and responsibility are not to shape the group in the leader's own image but to see that the team lives out its covenantal agreements with Christ and the congregation at large and that team members live out their covenantal agreements with one another.

The team covenant specifies the basis for the formation of the ministry team and defines what a particular team's house of love will look like. What is the team's purpose? How will team members relate to one another? What kinds of obligations will they live by?

The basis on which people serve together in the church is covenantal love and commitment. Christians believe that the Spirit of God is present to bind people together in community. The covenant is a good, biblical way to form Christian community. It is absolutely essential that ministry teams and church leadership forge clear commitments and covenants in order to lead effectively.

Workplace Covenants

Innovators in organizational management have also realized the value and importance of covenants for creating meaningful work communities. Max De Pree and Roger Schwarz are examples of contemporary organizational thinkers whose work dovetails with this discussion about perichoretic ministry teams. The research and practical applications of such management innovators can be helpful to ministry teams seeking specific ways to build covenantal community.

Max De Pree (1989), for example, reminds us that business and organizational covenants founded on rules alone are cold. The goal of the covenant is not to delineate specific behaviors in such a way that the agreement feels like a straight jacket. Rather the covenant is meant to give order to passion, to set forth respectful and honorable ways of living forth one's heartfelt love.

> Covenantal relationships . . . induce freedom, not paralysis. A covenan-tal relationship rests on shared commitment to ideas, to issues, to val-ues, to goals, and to management processes. Words such as love, warmth, personal chemistry are certainly pertinent. Covenantal rela-tionships are open to influence. They fill deep needs and they enable work to have meaning and to be fulfilling. Covenantal relationships reflect unity and grace and poise. They are an expression of the sacred nature of relationships.
>
> Covenantal relationships enable corporations to be hospitable to the unusual person and unusual ideas. Covenantal relationships toler-ate risk and forgive errors. I am convinced that the best management process for today's environment is participative management based on covenantal relationships [pp. 60–61].

Covenants in the workplace also can help members of a highly dys-functional group discover a way of working together that is productive and builds good community.

Roger Schwarz (1994) emphasizes using written *ground rules* to define group behavior that is supportive and helpful, as opposed to behavior that damages the group process. Such ground rules can resemble a form of covenant or contract. The following five items, defining how healthy groups interact, are examples from a number of useful ground rules Schwarz has accumulated from a variety of sources (p. 75).

- Share all relevant information.
- Focus on interests, not positions.
- Disagree openly with any member of the group.
- Discuss undiscussable issues.
- All members are expected to participate in all phases of the process.

Schwarz (1994) also provides a very helpful analysis of group process and the way a team leader can help a team come to a place of covenantal agreement that can help it be more productive and healthy.

The Importance of Covenanting Leaders

Churches around the country are beginning to discover the value of implementing various kinds of covenants to form the basis for the members of church ministry teams to work together. I have heard some argue that covenants, whether verbal or in writing, are not needed. Church staffs, it is said, already know that they should behave according to the Gospel. It is offensive, they say, to set forth ground rules or covenantal guidelines as a way to define working relationships.

In my experience, however, and that of many others, healthy, teamlike conduct is not readily practiced on church staffs and other ministry groups. The *intent* to live the Gospel in relationships can be present, but the actual *doing of it* falters. One reason is that we are all sinners saved by grace, and we sometimes act in selfish, destructive ways. In most cases, however, teams have relational problems not because of a single culprit acting intentionally but because of dysfunctional behavior that goes unrecognized and unaddressed. Covenants help solve this problem by giving team members standards of good group behavior and relationships. Israel was supposed to live out its covenant with God *in love*. Ministry teams, also, can use covenants to define loving relationships and what they look like, with the master image of God in perichoresis forming the background for establishing covenant community.

Some church leadership teams operate according to a kind of verbal covenant encouraged by the pastor or other group leader. Buford Karraker has been leading Northwest Church in Fresno, California, for thirty years but has never needed to put a team covenant in writing. "We say it all the time," he told me. "We cram into my office until we're hanging from the rafters, and then we say where we are going, and what we are doing, and what we need from each other, and how we're going to get there, and what we expect from each other. We don't need to write it down."

Gene Appel at Central Christian Church in Las Vegas, Nevada, told me something similar. Worship attendance at Central Christian has grown in twelve years from 450 to more than 3,700. "Used to be the whole staff could fit in a booth at a local restaurant," said Appel. "It was a lot easier back then. But trust is still a high point for us. My relationships with my staff team are built on trust and that is the working covenant we use."

Other teams and pastors, however, find written covenants to be more helpful. Jey Deifell, pastor of one of New England's largest churches, First

Church of Christ in Wethersfield, Connecticut, has a different approach. "It's very important to put the covenant in writing," he told me. "I came to this church from another one, which at one time had dysfunctional staff. I've learned that church staff members all need to be on the same track together. So one of the first things I did when I came to First Church was to go on retreat with the staff. Together we wrote a covenant. We *all* authored it. The group input was key. The covenant has helped us stay and grow together. We're a high octane staff that needed the specifics listed in the covenant."

Years ago I went through a period of staff conflict while pastor of Covenant Presbyterian Church in Austin, Texas. Some staff members left during that time. (It was the hurt and pain of that conflict that prompted me to begin my research on staff management in large churches which in turn led me to the subject of this book, forming team covenants that describe perichoretic fellowship.)

With the conflict fresh in everyone's mind, I engaged the staff in a process of writing a staff covenant to describe the kind of perichoretic fellowship among leaders we hoped to build. We held a retreat and several follow-up meetings, and these times were full of honest, vulnerable sharing as we worked to create the covenant. After several revisions, we had a document we could all approve and sign. (This covenant is reproduced in the Resource at the end of the book). Our covenant significantly reduced the level of staff tension and conflict. It also provided a model of team ministry that went beyond the staff to influence the other leaders in the congregation. In fact, the session (board of elders) eventually eliminated all church committees (amazing for Presbyterians!) and formed instead *ministry teams* throughout the congregation. Committee chairpersons became *team leaders,* and the various ministry teams became more focused and hands-on in their various areas of ministry.

We revised and readopted our covenant annually. Over the following years, when the team handled difficult situations, team members would comment that "the covenant is working," meaning, "we are working through this problem on the basis of how we envisioned we would as set forth in the covenant."

This written covenant worked to reduce tension *after significant conflict had occurred*. Church leadership, however, can reduce the possibility of ever reaching that level of conflict by establishing covenants earlier. Although they do not guarantee peace (covenants are effective only if people keep them), they can go a long way toward reducing relational problems among sincere leaders who are determined to live them.

Building Covenanting Teams

Here are some practical ways ministry teams can form covenants. Forming a covenant, whether written or verbal, ought to be step one in building leadership teams. If a team does not have *any* sense of covenant, I question whether it can lead at all. These team covenants form the basis for community upon which all else is built.

Obtain Team Leader Commitment to the Covenant

Most ministry teams have a principal leader who is the pastor, an elder, or other designated church leader. The leader must initiate covenant making. (This leader may be the same person as the covenant facilitator, but if she is not, she must see that the covenanting process happens.)

In fact, the first step toward establishing any of the perichoretic attributes in a ministry team is that the team leader commits to making each attribute happen. Teams must have a leader, but the principal role of that leader is, paradoxically, taking the responsibility to initiate a team process that results in the giving away of responsibility.

At First Church of Appleton, for example, the senior pastor, as team leader, could begin building a more effective ministry team by taking responsibility for ensuring that the members of the principal leadership team begin to develop good working relationships with each other. He could make arrangements for the team to go on periodic retreats to establish a covenantal working arrangement, do team-building exercises, conduct vision-casting sessions (see Chapter Four), and plan ministry. And he could continually use the team meetings to remind team members of their commitments to one another. He could frequently refer to the covenant they have agreed to.

As time went on, the pastor would sense intuitively when the group was off track or working contrary to its covenantal agreements. He could work to understand group dynamics and help the team focus on Christ as the center of its life and ministry. He could help it articulate how it plans to live out its Christian commitment and what that commitment looks like specifically in terms of team member relationships and the covenant members have established with one another. He could initiate the use of certain songs, scriptures, and symbols representing the covenant in weekly team meetings.

When team tensions begin to rise, as they did between the youth ministry and the music ministry, the pastor could then be in a good position as team leader to address the situation quite specifically. Individual team members could also bring up any growing problem they see in the church. The pastor could draw out these problems, allow for the venting of strong feelings and frustrations, and then ask the team what specific things it can do to see that the fabric of the church is not hurt by the conflict. Further conversation could center around the goal of keeping the team covenant and around the things team members have to do to ensure that conflict does not get out of hand. Members could ask themselves, How can we model for the other leaders of the church ways to deal with conflict and frustration in the church? What can we do to show them the value and depth of our covenantal relationship?

Once its leadership team was united and, on the basis of its covenant love, refused to allow conflict to breach its trust and fracture the faith community, First Church would be far less likely to enter into significant disarray. In fact, the funding problem could actually provide an opportunity (a teachable moment) for the leadership team to model for the congregation healthy ways of dealing with frustration and disagreement.

The team leader, then, has a key role in bringing group members together initially to make a covenant with one another and in reminding them often of their covenant obligations. Along with other team members, the team leader monitors the group's living out of the covenant and specifically addresses, as they appear, individual concerns that threaten the team's house of love.

Allow Sufficient Time

We must be prepared to invest a significant amount of time to develop a covenant that truly reflects the hearts and minds of our particular ministry teams. The covenant I initiated (see the Resource) took scores of hours to produce. Some church teams build covenants with the help of an extended retreat designed for this purpose. The exact amount of time will vary depending on the kind of covenant formed.

Verbal covenants are always being formed and re-formed. The team leader takes time each week or month to verbally address covenantal agreements. The team acknowledges and rewards behavior that matches covenant expectations.

Written covenants may take months to produce because it is best to solicit input from everyone involved. The covenant may go through a variety of drafts before the team agrees on a final written form. Afterward, the team will refer to the covenant frequently and revise it as needed.

In the case of First Church, the senior pastor could have prevented significant conflict in the church if he had taken the time earlier to form covenantal relationships among the staff. Energy and time applied early make for smoother sailing through the troubled seas that inevitably arise later. Many team leaders find this point one of the most difficult: forming, nurturing, and maintaining covenantal relationships takes a big investment of time. But that investment can save significant pain and distress later.

Offer Honesty and Self-Disclosure

The best covenants are those forged through honest conversation about what works and does not work in human relationships. Self-assessment and critique is difficult but often results in team camaraderie that far surpasses team members' previous relationships. Once again, it is important for the team leader to model self-disclosure and honesty. She sets the tone for the others to follow.

At First Church of Appleton the team could meet to share frustrations. The associate pastor for youth ministry could share honestly his objection to the music ministry budget increase. The team would then have to do the hard work of sorting out its priorities, sensing the priorities of the other leaders of the church, and forging an understanding of the funding issue at stake. If the team decided the funding imbalance was appropriate, then it could defuse congregational upset by saying so publicly. Conversely, if the team felt an injustice had occurred, members could agree, on the basis of their covenant, to suggest various remedies to the funding authority (or to change the funding themselves, if they have such responsibility). It may end up at First Church that the leadership team objects to the board of elders' funding priorities but that this objection is overruled by the elders. In this case, an opportunity presents itself, in which the team could model for the elders how to behave responsibly when "losing" a vote, as specified in the team covenant either implicitly or explicitly.

Resolutions to relational and organizational problems such as these begin with open, genuine sharing among team members.

Acknowledge Sin

It is important that we acknowledge our sinfulness when establishing our covenant relationships. We have a wonderful ally for covenant making in the doctrine of sin. We can freely acknowledge our need for grace and the fact we sometimes act out of pride, excessive ego, and selfishness. Because we understand sin, we should be able to recognize that we often act out of fear and anxiety rather than trust. Our covenants must be built on the basis of God's grace and not our self-sufficiency or perfection. Making provision for our confession to one another of our mistakes and for the giving and receiving of forgiveness enriches covenant relationships and creates safe community.

Neely Towe, pastor of the vital, vibrant Stanwich Congregational Church in Greenwich, Connecticut, believes that confession and honesty before God are key to relationships among leaders. "I guess the rubric of being trustworthy is repentance," she told me. "We need to be able to say to each other, 'I think I blew it'; 'I overreacted'; 'I let something go I shouldn't have.' Vulnerability and honesty are key in leadership."

Before their major disagreements started, First Church of Appleton staff could have forged a covenant acknowledging that sin is a problem in human relationships and how easy it is for egos to flare up and for people to feel anxious that they might not get what they need to do ministry. At the meeting when the growing problem between the youth and music ministries emerged, the team could then have called attention to the ways sin can drive such a problem and turn it into a crisis. Specifically, team members could ask, "How do we keep pride at bay in a situation like this without also simply standing by and letting an injustice occur? How does one assert that a error may have happened in funding without giving in to greed or thinking that one ministry is superior to another?" Prompted by the team's covenant, team conversation on the reality of sin and the ways sin manages to be highly destructive in conflicts would keep the team focused on not letting conflict get out of control. The team could then pray to God for help in controlling sin and for unity against that which has such great potential of ruining the team's house of love.

Be Specific

Covenants should avoid minutia. A covenant is not the place for rules such as "we agree not to drink the last of the coffee without refilling the pot." It is important, nonetheless, for us to be specific about behaviors that define good working relationships. For example, the five ground rules listed earlier (Schwarz, 1994) identify essential behaviors for working teams. (Notice that they are stated positively, as things to do rather than things to avoid: for example, "Share all relevant information," not, "Don't withhold information others need to know.")

The First Church of Appleton staff could have lessened the impact of their conflict with a covenant that specified certain behaviors. For example, their covenant might have specified, "We covenant to work out our problems as a team, settle our disputes among ourselves, and seek help from others when needed to resolve our differences, in order to represent our ministry to the congregation as the work of a united team." When the leadership team is united, it is far more likely the congregation will be as well.

Review Often

We should not put a covenant on a shelf somewhere and produce it only when there is a problem. We should review it often; revise and rewrite it as needed; reward team member behaviors that match it. We can print all or selected parts of the covenant on our team agenda. If the covenant is one page long, we can frame it for each team member and hang it in an obvious place in each office or hang the master copy in a conspicuous place in a central office. We can devise a symbol that represents the covenant and put the symbol in places where the team gathers for coffee. We can work to remind each other why the covenant is important and what it requires of each of us.

The staff at First Church of Appleton could have remained more focused and determined to work out their relational problems if they had previously covenanted to do so and were reminded of their covenant often. Their team meetings would not be for one hour every other week, but for two or three hours each week, with perhaps a longer meeting with a meal once a month. The covenant they forged could be reread, portions could be taught weekly, readings (for example, from Edwin Friedman's *Generation to Generation,* 1985) relevant to key points of the covenant could be assigned by the senior minister or team leader, and a song related to the covenant might be sung. These frequent reminders could have prepared First Church staff to avoid anger and resolve the conflict responsibly.

Orient New Team Members

As new members come into a team, the covenant can orient them to their new ministry. I have distributed a team's covenant to *potential* new team members, making sure they understand in advance what will be asked of them. However their orientation is managed, we should make sure that new team members understand and take ownership of the team covenant.

Once First Church of Appleton had agreed on a staff covenant, it could make sure that all staff were familiar with it. After all, the covenant would not matter if, say, the music director were a late hire who was never asked to read the covenant or informed about the traditions of the church staff and the core values they share. But how could that music director even begin to consider joining the First Church leadership team if he did not know the most important commitments of the team? How could the team be assured that the music director would honor the team covenant if he had not had a chance to express his commitment explicitly *before* being hired? Too often, churches hire staff members because of their credentials and experience but fail to do the important work of determining values and commitments and determining whether or not potential team members are aligned with church and leadership team commitments.

Distribute Widely

When there are a number of teams within a church and each team has agreed on a covenant, the church can accumulate these covenants into one booklet and make it available to everyone. These covenants are models for others to follow. If a church has only one covenant forged by its principal leadership team, it should still distribute it widely throughout the church. Distributing covenants beyond the ministry teams does two things. First, it offers a helpful model of healthy community to others. Second, it helps team members honor and abide by their covenantal agreements, because they know that people outside the team are aware of their commitments. It is easier, for example, for a team member to honor the covenant proviso to "speak well of your fellow team members to other people" when she knows that the entire congregation is aware she has made a commitment to do so.

If First Church of Appleton had had a staff covenant and the elders had received it and read it, they would have been in a position to call attention to that covenant and its agreement that staff would not engage in the kind of behavior exhibited by both the youth and music directors when they fanned the emerging conflict over funding and made it highly public. Invariably, elders get caught up in such conflicts as well. The shared covenant would have worked at First Church to inhibit the conflict and thus the elders' involvement; it would have called upon all the principal leaders of the church to act responsibly. The conflict would have been isolated, limited to a few and prevented from doing much damage, if such a covenant had existed and had been widely known.

Be Gracious

Covenants designed to help people live by healthy, spiritual standards may be difficult for some team members to follow. Many individuals' dysfunctional behavior has been rewarded and encouraged for many years. It may take time and patience to work through the many ways team members may break their covenant promises. Team members must be patient with one another. They must identify better ways to work together; constantly reward and encourage appropriate behavior; tell each other what was helpful and what was not helpful. They must recognize that it may take some people longer than others to get on board. They must remember that God is patient with us.

Before the First Church of Appleton leadership team, having lived through the conflict described at the beginning of this chapter and having agreed to create a covenant, could forge that covenant, the team members would have to work at forgiving one another for the previous dispute. Our covenants with one another are founded on grace. We enter into such agreements very much aware of our own need for grace and in a conscious attempt to live grace out in relationships.

Thus the First Church staff might have recognized that it had been the habit of the youth director to engage laypeople in disputes that should be worked out within the leadership team. If, instead of having the senior minister take him aside for a private talk, the team then, *as the leadership team,* had acknowledged this tendency with the youth director, as difficult as this is, showing grace to him and encouraging him to grow, it would have increased its strength as a leadership team. Future acknowledgment of the youth director's improvement and success at being a faithful team member would further encourage team members' ability to deal honestly with one another and to grow in their ability to relate well with another, as inspired by Christ.

This kind of "life together," as Dietrich Bonhoeffer (1954) described it, is difficult, but exceedingly rewarding.

4

THE VISIONARY TEAM

EFFECTIVE MINISTRY teams are those that cast a vision that unites people around a God-given cause. Visionary teams are motivated by a strong sense of mission and purpose. They know where they are going and work to align their energy and effort toward fulfilling their divinely inspired purpose. The mission of the ministry team is contagious. It attracts those who confirm that the mission is not simply humanly devised but is a vision from God for meaningful service. It is imperative that the principal leadership team of a church have a strongly focused vision *for* the congregation that is correspondingly affirmed and lived out *by* the congregation. It is also important, however, that all the ministry teams of a particular church have a specific sense of mission that is unique to their own activity and yet fits within and supports the larger vision for the whole congregation.

Tents of Ministry

First Church of Appleton, as described in Chapter Three, was organized around *tents,* or centers, of ministry. These ministry centers acted semi-autonomously, had separate constituencies with their own staff, leaders, and budgets, and tended to compete with each other for funding and space, which sometimes resulted in the kind of conflicts shown earlier between the youth and music ministries. In addition, the various ministries at First Church had various missions and visions. Each area's focus on its own mission encouraged it to regard itself as separate from the others. They had never discussed whether there might be a larger single vision to which they might all agree.

A ministry team with a covenantal relationship is less likely than the First Church ministries were to support conflict between ministry areas, and it also has the ability to dissolve conflict on the basis of the healthy, spiritually based relationship standards the team members have set and modeled. Yet even though a covenanting ministry team is more likely to fend off the worst effects of conflicts and fractures in congregations by creating biblical patterns of relationships, it does not eliminate the organizational dynamic that created the various camps in the first place. Thus, unless First Church attends to the organizational problem that is fragmenting the church, its staff will continue to spend much time trying to hold together ministry areas that are prone to pull apart or the ministry areas will simply become dominated by the one with the strongest leadership, that is, a hierarchy will be confirmed.

Although even the smallest congregation can be fragmented into ministry centers that eventually compete and even war with each other, the medium-sized to large churches are especially susceptible. Over and over I have observed how a small congregation will grow larger, hire staff to manage sprawling new programs, see various tents of ministry emerge, and then find these ministry centers beginning to wander from the fold.

One solution to this problem was suggested by a colleague when he remarked to me that "the best way to avoid having renegade small groups who run off to start their own churches or join another is not to form them in the first place." This argument is remarkably common. It is easier not to grow than to grow. But for those who continue to think that the Great Commission is still a mandate from the Savior to be obeyed and that ministry is something to be taken out into the world with passion, this suggestion is not acceptable. Vibrant, growing churches need not curb their outreach in fear of revolt and fragmentation. Instead each church can build significant unity in itself, to preserve its peace as it broadens its outreach.

The Drawstring: Vision Casting

Churches with ministry areas loosely held together and competing with one another need a strong common vision to unite them. That vision is the overarching goal and purpose of the church. A general mission statement is not enough. Nearly every church has some kind of mission statement that is so generally worded that it would fit any church. Certainly any church is united under the same Lord, the same Baptism, the same Spirit, and the same biblical purposes as any other church. And it is helpful to be reminded from time to time of what Presbyterians call *The Great Ends of the Church*. Nevertheless, individual congregations must go further and articulate clearly what it is God *uniquely* calls them to be and do.

The vision is like a drawstring that pulls the organization together and focuses it on its particular mission. The energy, spiritual gifts, resources, and organizational structure of the church are aligned with the vision. Youth, music, children's, singles', and other ministries of the congregation become centered around the common calling. Leaders no longer fight for what each one needs in a particular area of ministry but rather ask how their ministry area is working to fulfill the larger vision. In this fashion, the congregation becomes more like what Rick Warren (1995) describes as a *purpose driven church*.

Denny Bellesi, pastor of Coast Hills Community Church in Aliso Viejo, California, says this is what having a vision did for his congregation. "I planted the church thirteen years ago," he told me. "When there were only two hundred to three hundred coming to worship, we could manage it easily. The staff was tight knit. There was not much structure." Then the church began to grow. And growth created complexity and complications: "We started hiring people like me. They were entrepreneurs who could start new ministries. But we didn't know what to do with them. In those days we used to put up tents. But we were not sure we were all contributing to the same thing. We had lots of activity, but not much synergy. And every time we set up another new ministry, we actually risked losing the synergy that contributed to our vitality. If you don't have a common theme, then you are creating churches within churches."

Bellesi then realized the need for an infrastructure that would pull all of the ministries together. That infrastructure began with a uniting vision. "The vision becomes the starting point. You first have to know where you are going. It is absolutely essential. After determining your mission, your vision for ministry, then you begin to rally the people and resources to fulfill that mission."

The team-based church is a vision-driven church that is pulled together by a strong focused purpose.

Biblical Visions

In the Bible we see people and whole faith communities motivated and inspired by a clear vision from God. Moses was a middle-aged man who was content with the quiet life of a shepherd in the pastoral valleys of Midian when God burst into his life with a mission. He was afraid and resistant at first, but he had no doubt what God was asking him to do. He was called by God for a specific mission that had a clear demand upon his life.

The people did not follow Moses because they thought he had a good idea. The people followed Moses because they sensed that God truly sent him, that his mission was God inspired. They believed that God was behind the mission, and so they followed the one who articulated *God's* call.

Jeremiah was a young man who was likely terrified with the prospect of confronting his elders (Jer. 1:7–8) and yet God called him to a mission and assured him that he would have what he needed to carry it out. The mission was like a "fire in his bones" that could not be doused. Jeremiah lived it with conviction and determination even though it required of him great effort and suffering.

Mary was faced with the prospect of a problem pregnancy, but an angel assured her that the child she would carry, conceived by the Spirit, was of God and for God's purposes. This divine assurance gave her the courage and tenacity to face what must have been intense social embarrassment. Mary endured much because she was convinced that her mission was from God. She had a unique role to play, and she was willing to play it.

Paul was clear that he was the apostle to the Gentiles and not the Jews. Although much of his ministry included Jews, he felt especially equipped and called by God to go into Gentile lands with the saving Gospel of Jesus Christ. This was his vision, his specific contribution for the spread of the Gospel, and, by God's grace, he was determined to do it.

These biblical people are only a sampling of many in Scripture who endured much, gave much, lived much, hoped much, and enjoyed much because they were convinced of their specific calling to live for God and do God's will.

The heroes and heroines of the Bible are often individual leaders with a mission who live it out with faith and conviction and draw others to follow. There are, however, examples in Scripture of visionary teams and communities, where the focus is not on a specific leader but on the effort of the group to fulfill a divine mission. This is not to say these communities of faith are without leaders. But they are team oriented rather than leader oriented. One such example can be found in Mark, chapter two, which tells how a team of people (at least four) had the conviction, vision, unity, and determination to take their ailing friend to Jesus for healing.

First, notice there is no mention of a particular leader.

> When [Jesus] returned to Capernaum after some days, it was reported
> that he was at home. So many gathered around that there was no
> longer room for them, not even in front of the door; and he was

speaking the word to them. Then some people came, bringing to him
a paralyzed man, carried by four of them [1–3].

This team of four is convinced that Jesus could help their friend. The
people in the team had to learn to walk together carrying a heavy object
and agree on the route to Jesus' house. Reaching the house, they met the
obstacle of the crowd preventing their entry. At this point we might have
thought they had done enough, made a valiant effort, and showed sin-
cerity and collegiality in getting their friend to the house. But they are not
satisfied with less than total success in their mission. They display dili-
gence and a sense that they are on a sacred mission.

> And when they could not bring him to Jesus because of the crowd,
> they removed the roof above him; and after having dug through it,
> they let down the mat on which the paralytic lay [4].

The creative team comes up with a solution. At the top of the roof,
with the hole dug, where does the rope come from? The people of this
team are not only innovative but resourceful, coming up with the tools
they need to accomplish the cause. Jesus is impressed.

> When Jesus saw their faith, he said to the paralytic, "Son, your sins
> are forgiven" [5].

When Jesus saw *their* faith, the man's sins were forgiven. At this point
in the narrative, there is no evidence of the paralytic's faith. The effort and
conviction of the community that brought him to Jesus is acknowledged,
and Jesus pardons the man's sins. Later, the paralytic would have an opportunity to demonstrate his own faith response to Jesus' healing words:

> "I say to you, stand up, take your mat and go to your home." And he
> stood up, and immediately took the mat and went out before all of
> them; so that they were all amazed and glorified God, saying, "We
> have never seen anything like this!" [11–12].

These four men who carried their friend on the mat had to learn to
walk together carrying a heavy object, agree on the pathway to the house
where Jesus was teaching, overcome the obstacle of finding no clear entry
into the house, be innovative in their solution to the problem by getting

their hands dirty, and secure necessary resources such as the rope. What was their motivation to go through all this trouble? They had a strong and clear vision that Jesus could heal their friend.

We need today such visionary teams, who help congregations be clear about the specific mat they can carry to bring the broken of our world to Jesus. A sharp, specific vision is required that enables individuals to join in taking up their end of the mat. That vision becomes their focus and not a specific leader. This is the kind of vision the twenty-first century church needs to give witness to Jesus Christ in a postmodern world.

Perichoresis and Vision

I have noted that although there is no developed doctrine of the Trinity in Scripture, it is nonetheless clear in many Bible verses that God is revealed to us as Father, Son, and Spirit. Some things can be inferred from this holy fellowship of God. For example, God the Father, Son, and Spirit is not passive. In creation, the love of the fellowship of this one God in three persons brimmed and flowed, and God created all that is. God spoke all things into being. "God said, 'Let there be light,' and there was light." These were intentional, active endeavors of God that indicate meaning and purpose. God had a vision of what would be and whom God would create to share love and fellowship. Creation was not random, but the acting out of the love of God in purposeful, visionary activity.

Karl Barth argued in his *Church Dogmatics* (1957) that God is not speculated about simply existentially; in other words, the point is not simply that God exists. Rather, God's existence is always understood by Christians in the context of God's revelation to us, particularly through Jesus Christ. God's revelation to us is active and purposeful. Even though God is not equated with God's revealed works, nonetheless "in His works He is Himself revealed as the One He is" (p. 260). Barth went on to say, "What God is as God, the divine individuality and characteristics, the *essentia* or 'essence' of God, is something which we shall encounter either at the place where God deals with us as Lord and Saviour, or not at all" (p. 261). God, then, is known to us in God's activity with us. This activity is revealed to us with purpose and intent. It is specific, gracious and redemptive.

Ministry with vision, purpose, love, and passion imitates God's creative and redemptive activity. Ministry teams are drawn into the fellowship of God and the members unto one another that they might know the love of

God and then translate it into meaningful activity. Andrei Rublev hoped that his brethren would find fellowship with God and one another by concentrating on the image of the perichoretic fellowship of the Trinity. This house of love was not meant to be a spiritual retreat from the world's turmoil, but rather "a way to keep their hearts centered in God while living *in the midst* of political unrest" (Nouwen, 1987, p. 20).

Visionary teams act with passion and purpose. They wish their own fellowship to be extended and broadened to include others. They act out of grace and pour out grace because God has been gracious to them. They seek to live the redemption that has been won for them on the cross. These teams are intentional and filled with God-inspired purpose that ignites them to pursue a cause.

Our Cultural Hunger for Purposeful Living

There is a hunger in contemporary society for *meaningful and spiritual activity.* People feel empty of purpose. They wonder why they are here. There exists today a cultural quest for ultimate meaning.

The church does not inspire vision-driven leadership *because* culture is receptive to it. We recognize, rather, that God acts with purpose and that this attribute is reflected in visionary ministry teams and can be linked to the postmodern trend of seeking meaningful and purposeful activity. Postmodern individuals respond better to churches with a cause than to churches that have no clarity of mission. This cultural trend can help the church reform itself upon a strong scriptural basis.

We see the hunger in contemporary society for meaningful, benevolent activity in many ways. For example, at one of my wife's annual Christmas barbecues for the staff of the pediatric clinic where she used to work, I found myself sitting next to the husband of one of the nurses, and I became intensely interested in what he was telling me.

"I am excited to go to work every morning," he said, with a smile, and a gleam in his eye.

"Tell me why," I invited.

"I work for Acme Micro Design, and they have changed the way they operate. It used to feel like I was working for a big, impersonal company. The goal was production, production, production. And we were constantly worried about the bottom line. But the attitude has changed at work. The company has taken on a new way of operating and I love it."

"What specifically changed for you?"

"My manager has encouraged me to think differently about what I do. He has emphasized that our work group's primary goal is to make our clients successful. Instead of thinking first that I work for AMD, I am a partner with my customers. I am on their side, and I can help them do what they need to do to be successful in life."

"And this is what has changed your attitude about work?"

"Exactly! Oh, AMD still worries about the bottom line. And my paycheck comes from them. But now I feel like I am making a difference in the lives of our clients. I'm not just a peon in a corporation. I help people achieve their goals. And the company benefits from my service to others."

"Remarkable!" I thought. All kinds of lights lit up in my mind. How often we in the church try to get people to serve the institution of the church. Whether they be paid staff or volunteers, we have a position with a job description for them to do: perform this task that the organization needs done and get in return a paycheck or a vague sense that you are doing your duty to God. But do the people we recruit have a larger vision of how their contribution of work makes a difference in the lives of people? Can the secretary or custodian in our church say he partners with the whole staff to help people experience God in their lives? Does the worship usher know that what she is doing makes a difference for the Kingdom of God?

Workplace Vision Casting

There is a consensus among innovative organizational and business thinkers today that *leaders cast a vision that unites people around a cause.* Without that vision, people have no direction, no inspiration, and no meaning given to their work. Secular organizational leaders recognize that people need these things to work well and thrive in a corporate environment. It is absolutely critical, they argue, for a leader or leadership team to articulate the vision of the work group, give it sharp focus, and rally resources toward meeting that goal.

James Kouzes and Barry Posner make a strong case for the importance of vision casting in their best-seller, *The Leadership Challenge* (1995). Based upon significant research into the lives of successful leaders and the organizations they serve, Kouzes and Posner conclude: "The overwhelming consensus was that, without vision, little could happen. All enterprises or projects, big or small, begin in the mind's eye; they begin with imagination and with the belief that what's merely an image can one day be made real" (p. 93). Not everyone they interviewed called this focus a vision. "Some referred instead to *purpose, mission, legacy, dream, goal, calling,* or *personal agenda.* No matter what the term, though, the intent was the same: leaders want to do something significant, to accomplish something that no one else has yet achieved" (p. 94; emphasis added).

The young man I met at the staff party had been inspired to partner with clients for their success. This idea, this vision, stirred his imagination, and now he feels as though his work has meaning. Every day he is working with specific customers about their unique problems and how AMD services and equipment can help solve these problems. The critical element in his new enthusiasm for his work is his team's new vision of work as serving the needs of the customer so the customer can succeed rather than serving the needs of the corporation so the corporation can pay higher dividends to its investors.

Note, too, that even though AMD has a vision statement that includes service to the customer, that statement by itself was not a motivating factor for this employee. Similarly, James Collins and Jerry Porras (1994) point out that simply having a vision statement is not a guarantee that a company will become a *visionary company.* This man's dedication to his work turned positive only when he saw his manager and others on his team actually *doing* what the vision statement said and *reaffirming* one another as they sought to help their customers.

Nearly every church has a mission statement. It may be unique to that congregation or held in common among several churches in a single denomination. Simply having this vision statement is not enough. The key ingredient is a leadership team that lives the vision, breathes it, models it, tells its story any chance it gets, sleeps and eats it, and otherwise calls people together around it.

In the Christian community, George Barna has been writing about the importance of vision casting for church leaders. He reports (Barna, 1992) that in evaluating churches that are growing and healthy and those that are stagnant or in decline, one of the key distinctions that emerges is the existence of a true vision for ministry: "In every one of the growing, healthy (that is, user-friendly) churches I have studied, there is a discernible link between the spiritual and numerical growth of those congregations and the existence, articulation, and widespread ownership of God's vision for ministry by the leaders and participants of the church. Conversely, there is invariably a clear absence of vision in those congregations in which there is neither spiritual nor numerical growth taking place. Rarely in my research do I find such overt, black-and-white relationships" (p. 12).

Postmodern people are looking for something meaningful around which to order their lives. They are hungry for truth and seeking that which is ultimately important and worthy of their energy. The church is in a wonderful position to feed the hungry with the truth of God, and visionary teams must lead the charge.

Building Visionary Teams

A church leadership team can create a covenant among its members apart from the congregation (and, as I have suggested, as a model for the congregation); however, it is impossible for a church team to work as a vision-driven team in isolation from the congregation's sense of purpose. There must be a unity of vision among the members of the leadership and the members of the congregation for the ministry to be effective. More specifically, building a visionary team cannot be separated from building a visionary congregation. Therefore the suggestions that follow focus on inspiring *both* the team and congregation toward highly purposeful activity.

Commit to Seek the Vision

Whether the team leader initiates the vision-seeking process himself or whether he is encouraged to do so by the leadership team, elders, or congregation at large, he must be committed to making it happen or it will not be successful. It is also imperative that the principal team leader (usually the pastor or senior pastor in a given congregation) be the advocate for the process. It is very difficult for leadership teams to initiate the process if the team leader is opposed to the idea or gives little energy to the effort.

At First Church of Appleton the senior pastor is in an ideal position to recognize the damage done by competing ministries and to call the church together for prayer and reflection on how to pull the ministries together under a common banner. His commitment and leadership toward building that uniting vision are critical. People in key leadership roles must use their responsibility and authority to lead the congregation through a process of determining the congregation's unique cause. The focus of the church during this time should not be on the pastor leader but on the vision of God discerned by the pastor and congregation through a vision-seeking process.

Seek the Mission of the Church

A leadership team and congregation might arrive at a specific mission, or vision, for their church in a variety of ways. What should not happen is that the principal church leader randomly invents a vision or draws it out of a hat or tries one that worked well in a church in another state. Although a vision can have a variety of immediate sources, all church visions should have the Spirit of God as their ultimate source.

Some pastors can discover the vision without involving the leadership team. Terry Fullam, formerly of St. Paul's Episcopal Church in Darien, Connecticut, received the vision for his ministry and for his congregation at St. Catherine's Church at the foot of Mount Horeb. Others take the congregation through a lengthy, inductive process of determining what it is God is calling the church to be and do. Still other pastors work principally with their key leadership teams to discern the vision, then try it out on the elders, and then on the congregation at large. But however the vision comes, the principal leaders and the main core of the congregation just *know* when the vision is from God and worthy of their full commitment.

A newly developed church does well to have a strongly articulated vision that has been discerned by the pastor. Everyone who joins the church is from the very beginning committed to that singular purpose. Saddleback Church, described in Pastor Rick Warren's *The Purpose Driven Church* (1995), is a good example of a start-up church that began with a strong focus. Driven by this purpose, the congregation attracted those who confirmed that vision and repelled those who objected to it (later in this chapter I deal with the criticism that a purpose-driven church may be too exclusive). Pastors of existing, traditional congregations need to work harder and longer with their leadership and members to arrive at a clearly articulated, specific purpose. Although the process usually takes longer, the result is quite similar: a leadership team and congregation that are sharply focused for ministry. Whether a congregation is brand-new or hundreds of years old, it needs to know specifically what God would have it do.

THE LEADER RECEIVES AND ARTICULATES THE VISION. Churches that develop their visions from the top down, with the pastor articulating the vision first and then seeking support, should not be categorized offhand as hierarchical. Intuitive leaders can sense the gifts and orientations of a congregation and begin to express them in specific language. The principal leader of the church thereby uses her gifts to bless the church with the articulation of the vision. This may, however, not be the exact mission statement the congregation ends up with. The leader may first articulate the vision and then send it out for review and amendment. The process can be imagined as a series of loops, with the leader first articulating the vision then getting it affirmed by the principal leadership team, which returns it with either full acclamation or with amendment. Then the vision loops around the larger set of leaders in the church for affirmation and review, and they send it back with affirmation or amendment. Then it loops out to the congregation who pray about it, reflect on it, and send it back with their reactions. So a process that began as leader initiated and leader articulated can become consensus building, taking in the whole congregation and its leadership, and affirming the vision as indeed God's will for the whole church.

An example of a church leader who began the vision process with his own articulation of the mission is Scott Farmer, pastor of Community Presbyterian Church in Danville, California. Instead of independent leaders and competing ministry areas, Community Presbyterian has a leadership team with a clear purpose that unites members into a highly cohesive staff. This unity of purpose extends beyond the staff to the congregation and even into the city.

Community Presbyterian Church is located in northern California's San Ramon Valley, which has a population of about 100,000 people. Under Farmer's leadership, the leadership team (made up of staff and elders) and congregation have set a clear goal they call the Ten Year Vision. "We are the catalyst for doubling the percentage of people of the San Ramon Valley who confess Jesus Christ as Savior and who are intentionally contributing to Kingdom causes," Farmer told me.

This sharply focused vision started with Farmer's own sense of where God was leading the congregation. First, he shared it with his principal leadership team who came to believe as well that this was God's will for their church. Then, Farmer and the team shared the vision with the session (the board of elders), who also came to believe that it was God's vision for their church. Then Farmer approached several churches in the valley to see if they would share this same vision. Eight other churches have signed on. "Our church's own goal is to increase the number of people we serve at this site 2.5 times," Farmer says. "However, we have stated that this growth cannot come from existing Christians. Only 15 percent of the valley is part of a church. That means we all have to reach out to the 85 percent that are left."

This uniting vision is not just stated at Community Presbyterian Church. Everything the church does is tied to it. Farmer explains that "part of every staff job description includes this goal. Since the vision includes other churches beyond our own, some staff time is dedicated to helping other churches in the valley grow. For example, we found that our youth group was not reaching youths from a particular junior and senior high school. So, we started a new church in the area to minister to them and develop a ministry in that area. We lent them money and staff time to help them develop their own youth program. Our children's department helped a Catholic church put on a vacation Bible school because we do that well. We had something we could teach them to help them grow. Our preschool has given two of our leading teachers and a director to help another church start a preschool." Farmer reports that church personnel assessments evaluate what each staff person is doing to contribute toward the goal. The church also measures the effectiveness of the congregation's whole ministry on the basis of this vision. "We have raised an extra million dollars just for this evangelism vision—we call it 'Mission Funding: People Meeting Christ.' Eventually, we hope to raise 3.3 million dollars."

Community Presbyterian Church is just one example out of the many churches with visionary teams who articulate the vision of God affirmed by and subscribed to by the congregation, resulting in strong, focused congregations that are making a difference in the communities they serve.

The leader who receives the vision and then leads others on the basis of it is often found in Scripture (think of Moses, for example, or Nehemiah), but that is not the only way God works to draw a congregation together under a common mission.

THE LEADERSHIP TEAM GUIDES THE CONGREGATION IN VISION SEEKING. A God-given mission for a particular congregation is sometimes the result of a process that *may* be initiated by the leader (at a minimum, it has his support and enthusiasm) but is carried out by the principal leadership team. That team may be the church staff, the board of elders, or another set of leaders recognized by the congregation as responsible for giving direction to the life and work of the church. This team engages in serious prayer and Bible study, seeking God's will for the direction of the church. Worship and prayer also play a key role as the congregation calls upon the Lord for guidance and discernment. The congregation is encouraged to pray for the leadership team, members of the church are encouraged to discuss their own thoughts and prayers for the vision, and one or more congregational meetings are held to gather members' thoughts and views.

A retreat is planned so the members of the leadership team can go away by themselves and seek out God's vision for the congregation through prayer, worship, and dialogue. Although the principal team leader must give spiritual leadership and encouragement for the process, the team itself arrives at the specific vision. In one process for reaching a shared vision, a meeting leader writes on a blackboard the vision elements proposed by team members who have paid careful attention to the thoughts and opinions of the congregation and who also take the unique history and culture of the church into account, along with the church's local community and any important social factors. When this *brainstorming* process is completed, the list of proposed vision elements is handed over to a writing team of one or two gifted people, who derive from these elements a sharply worded, brief but specific vision statement. This vision statement is returned to the entire group for further evaluation and prayer, until the all team members conclude that they have arrived at the specific mission for their congregation.

How long will the process take? It will take as long as it takes! Some pastors and teams agonize for months until they sense that God has given them the specific vision for their church. For others, the vision percolates up naturally through the prayer, worship, and dialogue that take place at the retreat. Although the vision-shaping process cannot be forced, if it takes too long, it can introduce considerable frustration and a sense that the church is floundering in the congregation at large (this is the chronic state of many churches that do not have a clear vision).

Make the Vision the Focal Point

Once the vision for a local congregation is discerned and articulated, we should plaster it everywhere! We can write it on the stationery, frame copies of it in an attractive format and hang it all over the church facilities, preach it, write about it in the newsletter, symbolize it with a gripping image that can continue to be linked to it, write lyrics about it and sing it, and make it part of the learning curriculum. That vision must become the ordering principle for the work of the church, and it is the leadership team that is primarily responsible for keeping the vision before the congregation. Just as the leadership team models covenant community in team relationships, it also models purposeful activity on the basis of the church's vision.

The vision statement is found all over the place at Coast Hills Community Church. It is on church stationery, recited at staff meetings, and displayed in prominent places. "You can't say the vision enough," Denny Bellesi told me. "You tell it over and over, in every group you can. We [the church staff] think people are getting bored hearing it over and over. But they're not. They need to be reminded of it constantly. So you have to keep saying it every chance you get. Tell it, retell it, then tell it again!"

The team-based church, then, is one that is motivated to act by the leadership team on the basis of a uniting vision. Because the congregation has come to own the vision through the process that generated it, the leadership team has a mandate both from God and from the people of God to order church life on the basis of it. The visionary team draws others into purposeful and spiritually meaningful activity on the basis of what the congregation discerns as its God-given cause.

Be Specific

One of the biggest mistakes churches make in forming vision statements is being too vague or general. There is a place for the general mission or confessional statement that unites the congregation to the work and ministry of other congregations. For example, First Church of Appleton might come up with a general mission statement something like this:

> The purpose of First Church is to be a community that glorifies God
> in worship, mission, education, and compassion.

That is a fine statement, but because it does not offer a specific cause for the congregation it will not engender the kind of support that an effective vision does. First Church can keep that statement as a general mission statement but it must follow it up with a vision statement like this:

> First Church of Appleton is committed to
> - *Worship,* that both feeds the believer and appeals to the
>   unbeliever
> - *Nurture,* that draws people into a closer discipleship with Jesus
>   Christ
> - *Mission,* that is enabled by the release of the spiritual gifts of its
>   members

The bullet points in the vision statement lend themselves to the development of specific action steps that will move toward vision fulfillment. The worship team can list specific ways it is both nurturing believers and appealing to unbelievers. It can also develop methods to test whether or not it is really doing these things. The same goes for the nurture and mission teams. They can easily build specific ministries based on this vision statement; ministries that can be easily evaluated.

The purpose statement of Saddleback Church employs alliteration (on the letter *m*) to help make its points memorable (Warren, 1995, p. 107):

> To bring people to Jesus and *membership* in his family,
> develop them to Christlike *maturity,*
> and equip them for their *ministry* in the church
> and life *mission* in the world,
> in order to *magnify* God's name.

Vision statements need not tell the whole story. Instead they should be catchy, memorable, clear, and focused.

A Common Objection to Vision Casting

At various conferences and events where I have presented these ideas about visionary leadership teams, I have heard this common objection: "How can a church be specific about its ministry without excluding people?" For example, a vision statement might say:

> Our church will reach out to the families of our community and help them stay together.

There are those who would object to this statement because it leaves out single people. My response, however, is that churches already have unwritten vision and mission statements that are exclusionary. These statements are found in each church's structures. In other words, a church might object to including the vision shown because it is exclusionary, *but the reality of its practice is that it does not intentionally reach out to single people anyway and has few in the congregation.* I find it curious that we want to keep our statements free from specifics and yet our practices of ministry are quite specific. We somehow think that if we do not specify that we want to help families that somehow more singles will come in the church door. But the nearby Second Church may actually have this in its vision statement:

> Our church will reach out to the single people of our community.

Churches are not everything to everyone in practice. Why not be clear about what it is we do well as a congregation, or feel called to do well, and celebrate that and let another congregation pick up where we leave off?

This is especially true when it comes to interracial ministry. Most mainline churches would say they are open to people of every race. Most mainline churches in the United States also have congregations that are nearly entirely white. We should be realistic and recognize that congregations are probably not going to attract people of other races unless they are intentional about reaching beyond racial boundaries. If they are, they might have this as part of a vision statement:

> Our church will reach out to the African American community of our
> city in mutual understanding.

They might then follow that phrase up with a strategic plan that outlines specific action steps to accomplish it. Some people will again object, saying that this vision statement excludes Hispanic people. But I would argue that a church should do just what it can at first, as it senses the Spirit leading it. It should really reach out to the African American community and then, if the Lord leads, it can add this to its vision later:

> Our church will reach out to multiethnic and racial groups in our city.

And it can devise specific ways to do that. The main thing is to understand what the church realistically can do, say it clearly, devise the strategy around the vision statement, then go and do it. If a congregation would do just that much, it would be much further along than one that is so vague and general in its convictions that nothing specific ever gets done.

Remember: Vision Is Not Enough

The leadership team that covenants together and works to articulate a common vision is in a wonderful *beginning* place. But the team has to follow through. Vision seeking is an absolutely essential beginning place, but by itself it is not enough.

"You begin with the mission," Denny Bellesi commented to me, "then create the systems to fulfill it." But he also issued an important warning. "For a while, everyone was writing vision statements, which is fine, but it's not enough. It's not enough simply to have a vision; you have to do something about it. You then have to do the hard work of developing your strategic plan off the vision. But the vision is essential to the process."

To sum up, then, church-based leadership teams must be covenantal in their love for God and one another. They must also have a clear vision, a sense of purpose that coincides both with God's will for their labor and the congregation's sense of the church's unique mission. The leadership team whose members have covenanted to work together as a house of love and that has a clear sense of purpose then sets out to create a culture that reflects that covenant and purpose.

5

THE CULTURE-CREATING TEAM

CHURCH LEADERS ARE called to create a culture that reflects the mission God calls them to do. Creating Christian culture in a church means developing the symbols, themes, activities, values, and structures that reinforce the faith and purpose of a given congregation. Ministry teams that make a difference in the world are inspired and equipped by the Spirit of God to shape these cultures.

Having a clear sense of a congregation's divine purpose and mission, the team then uses the rich tapestry of the church's symbols and narrative to reinforce that mission. New symbols, music, and images that naturally arise out of the congregation's history, or imported from other churches and adjusted for the local context, can be employed to reinforce the sense of mission for a congregation.

James Hopewell, an Episcopal priest, experienced the complexity of a church congregation when he pulled together a loosely formed group of people, gathered for worship, that grew into a vibrant and mature congregation. The growth of the church he attributed to God, but he also noted that certain social dynamics helped create a growing, thriving fellowship. He conducted a research project to learn more about the social dynamics of his congregation, and then expanded his study to include other congregations during a sabbatical year. "At the end of the year," he reports, "I concluded that a group of people cannot regularly gather for what they feel to be religious purposes without developing a complex network of signals and symbols and conventions—in short, a subculture—that gains its own logic and then functions in a way peculiar to that group" (1987, p. 5).

Congregations are cultures of their own that function within the larger culture of society. Although people of faith are hesitant to explain *everything* in purely sociological terms, it is nonetheless helpful to use sociological analysis as a way of discovering *how God works* and how we can join with God, who clearly desires to create good, faithful communities. Hopewell describes the rich and complex nature of the congregational culture as a river of narrative, symbol, and language: "Even a plain church on a pale day catches one in a deep current of narrative interpretation and representation by which people give sense and order to their lives. Most of this creative stream is unconscious and involuntary, drawing in part upon images lodged long ago in the human struggle for meaning. Thus a congregation is held together by much more than creeds, governing structures, and programs. At a deeper level, it is implicated in the symbols and signals of the world, gathering and grounding them in the congregation's own idiom" (p. 5).

Churches and their leadership teams need to be intentional about creating such cultures. The world around us is full of those who seek to persuade us by using culture-creating tools. Instead of abdicating this role to those who are more intentional about it than we are, we as church leaders must instead learn how to influence society more effectively with the Truth of God in Jesus Christ.

Going Beyond Generic

Effective culture-creating teams begin by first shaping their own team culture. How can they presume to begin to reinforce the church's mission with the congregation if, first, they have not created their own sense of culture that aligns with the vision? At First Church of Appleton the staff had only a vague idea of what they were supposed to be doing. They had their individual areas of responsibilities but no strong, clear uniting theme to pull them together and sharpen their focus and ministry. They have finally discerned their vision, but that is not enough. The next step is also crucial. Without it the vision will be nothing but black ink in a book somewhere. The next step the Appleton team must take is to form intentionally the culture that supports the vision of the church.

The leadership teams at Appleton must also understand that a generic Christian church culture is not enough. A generic church culture offers an ambiance of traditional Christian symbols, stained glass, an organ, pews, a narthex (lobby), and in many cases "reserved for clergy" parking signs. Generic church cultures are not "bad"; they simply do not communicate well to the postmodern world. They appear more and more to be irrelevant relics of a previous era.

Churches with a mission go beyond the generic Christian culture. Their specific vision or calling is found everywhere—in symbol, saying, picture, architecture, song, and printed materials. Rooms used by teams and staff have highly visual displays of the vision and related materials. Team agendas have the vision statement or a symbol for the vision printed at the top. More important, the vision and its attendant values and strategies are carried out in the activities of the church. Through both representations and actions, a typical church member has a clear idea of what the church is about, where it is going, and how he or she fits in.

The conflict at First Church of Appleton can be managed by a leadership team that covenants to model perichoretic fellowship. Their covenant love moderates the conflict in the congregation and provides a healthy spiritual context for working out the problems between competing ministries. The leadership team establishes its covenant, defining the nature of members' relationships, and then draws the congregation through a process that sharpens its sense of mission. Having determined the specific vision Christ has given for the congregation, the Appleton leadership team sets out to create a culture that reinforces that purpose.

In any church, culture-creating is at first the responsibility of the principal leadership team, which both creates the culture for its own team fellowship and expands it, drawing in other leaders and building the culture throughout the whole faith community. The first step the leadership team takes is to immerse its members in the symbols and themes of the culture and in living the culture. Then they can expand it to include the rest of the congregation.

Immersed in Egypt

Hollywood's DreamWorks studios offer an example of culture creating that reinforces an organization's purpose. In March 1997, DreamWorks (the film production company of Stephen Spielberg, Jeffrey Katzenberg, and David Geffen) invited groups of religious leaders to Hollywood to discuss the making of the movie *The Prince of Egypt,* based on the book of *Exodus.* I was in one of those groups that participated in a consultation with Jeffrey Katzenberg about the movie. We were also treated to a tour of one of the main DreamWorks facilities, and we were struck by the images representing the film that were displayed wherever we went. In the lobby of the main building, on the walls of the hallways, in the offices and conference rooms were constant reminders of the colors, music, camera angles, animation, and vocalization of the movie. The people in the Dream-Works *team* (the company does not use the term *employees*) came to work each day and, walking into the building, was immediately *immersed in ancient Egypt.* The filmmakers believed that the team was inspired and motivated by these constant reminders of the pharaohs' Egypt, that the animators, composers, artists, and technicians were better able to communicate the culture of ancient Egypt if, daily, they themselves were constantly reminded of the sun, sand, pyramids, and religious symbols of the land of the Nile. We observed that even the food servers in the cafeteria were immersed in the themes of Exodus.

Effective church-based leadership teams work to create a culture that reflects the values and mission of the reign of God. When a person walks into a church office, the building, setting, people, and surroundings all communicate. They tell an unspoken story of what is important to the church.

Years ago a search committee approached me about becoming the senior minister of the committee members' church. The church congregation worshiped in a beautiful, ornate cathedral-like building. The facility housed expensive art and furnishings imported from Europe. Several full-time security guards were on the church payroll. The sanctuary was formal and gothic. Yet a search committee member expressed bewilderment to me. He said that the church was in the third wealthiest county in the United States and it had on its membership roll CEOs of some of the nation's largest corporations. And yet, he said, the per capita giving of the congregation was less than that of the one I served in Austin, populated by people without nearly the same personal incomes. I told him the answer to that riddle was easy. People walk into the sanctuary of that ornate church and look around and think, "These folks don't need any money!" The church facility told a story of wealth. It also said that the building and its contents were high priorities. And people generally are not as motivated to give to keeping up a building, especially an affluent one, as they are to fulfilling a mission.

Culture creating takes the words of a church and moves beyond them to forge values and ways of being that reflect that church's core beliefs. The symbols, sayings, and images are not themselves the culture but depict the milieu being sought. The leadership team is principally responsible for generating the materials, symbols, and rituals that serve to develop the culture.

A Culture-Creating God

Throughout Scripture, we find God involved in culture creating. When God spoke everything into being and created Adam and Eve to roam about the Garden of Eden, a culture was formed that was "good." The environment signified God's providence, creativity, and love. The idyllic community portrayed in Genesis, chapter 1, is that of Adam and Eve living in perfect fellowship with God who "walked" with them in the garden. God made a wonderful world—a house of love—that reflected the perichoretic culture and community of the triune God.

Then sin entered the world and all that God made was marred. The beautiful culture shaped by God was twisted and corrupted as a result of humanity's sin. We became alienated from God as *rivals* to God, seeking to construct our own cultures, shaped in *our* image, as monuments of human pride.

God then set about to redeem and restore. Covenants initiated by God with us became the centers of new cultures, of worshiping communities, which sought to be restored to fellowship with God through worship and obedience. The Mosaic covenant that included the Ten Commandments, for example, became the center of Jewish faith—of Old Testament cultures—as a way of being reconciled back to God.

In the New Testament, Jesus modeled the house of love and exhorted his followers to live and show forth the culture of the Kingdom of God. He taught his disciples another way of living in the world, a way that formed the basis for a new community and new culture. In the Sermon on the Mount (Matt. 5–7), for example, Jesus taught his followers a radical new ethic running counter to the cultures of the Romans and Pharisaical Judaism. This new way of living is part of a larger ethos we might call the culture of the Church of Jesus Christ.

The cross became the central symbol of Christian faith. The gift of the death of the Son of God, an atonement for human sin, centered the Christian community upon sacrificial love. Along with the new ethic introduced in the teachings of Jesus, was a new language (for example, *body of Christ, people of the way, Lord's Supper, Christian baptism*), new structures (for example, deacons and evangelists), and a new network of relationships (churches) centered around a common *kerygma* (preaching) of the risen Lord. The gift of the Spirit of God transformed human beings and with them forged a new community, a new *Christian* culture, exemplified in new or adopted music, symbols, language, traditions, and convictions.

Within this larger context of the new Christian culture emerged congregations, each as a unique subculture. The Book of Revelation depicts seven congregations, which are exhorted, encouraged, and rebuked by the risen Lord. Each had its unique ministry and challenges. Founded upon the same principles and teachings of Christ, these churches had nonetheless specific ministries for them individually to pursue.

The Pauline epistles also show us the differences of various Christian communities that nonetheless shared a common Lord, faith, and overarching Christian culture. The language, traditions, symbols, and ministry of the Corinthian church differed from those of the congregation at Thessalonica, which were different from those at Ephesus. United under a common general faith and emerging Christian culture, each congregation nonetheless had a specific ministry for its particular location. Each unique church reflected its own cultural contexts and specific missions.

Scripture, then, reveals to us many ways in which God has been about the work of culture creating. First, in the overall sense of the creation of the universe. Then in the establishment of covenant communities, each representing a unique worshiping culture dedicated to the restoration of fellowship with God. The Christian church then emerged as a larger culture centered around the teachings, death, and resurrection of Jesus Christ. Within this larger Christian culture, specific Christian communities grew and witnessed to the risen Lord, depicting unique ways to spread the Word and live the faith, specific to their location and unique calling.

Culture creating by God and the people of God is not new. When it is Spirit driven, prayed for, and centered around a God-given vision, it has a powerful effect of uniting complex congregational dynamics into a vibrant fellowship. Thus the leadership team must be intentional about creating its own team culture as it also shapes the culture of a given congregation.

Perichoretic Culture

When Andrei Rublev painted his famous icon of the Trinity, he depicted many of the central symbols of Christian faith and culture, painting the persons of God in the context of images representing biblical narratives. These images are culture creating and reinforcing, grounding Trinitarian faith in biblical history and imagery. It is as if Rublev meant to say that God is known in God's activities, and these actions reveal and reflect the culture of God's very self. By immersing ourselves in these images of the salvific history of God, we immerse ourselves in God's very being.

In the upper-left corner of the Rublev icon is a building symbolizing the house of God as the world the Lord created. The tree in the center background represents the cross of Jesus. The round table shows the fellowship of the three persons, the cup has inside of it a tiny lamb representing the Sacrament, and the rectangle on the base of the table represents the four corners of the earth. Inside the rectangle, the L-shaped figure represents that the ones invited into this holy fellowship come by way of the narrow path. It is also interesting to note the order of the figures. I have shown this icon to many groups and asked them to tell me which one is the Father. Nearly everyone says the center figure, because it is taller and brighter than the other two. This is a typically Western way of thinking: the Father is on the top of the pyramid. Actually, the figures were painted in the order they are named in the Apostles' Creed: "I believe in the Father, the Son and the Holy Spirit. . . ." The center figure, the Son, was painted in sharper colors because it is he whom we have beheld as the only Son begotten of the Father.

> We declare to you what was from the beginning, what we have heard, what we have seen with our eyes, what we have looked at and touched with our hands, concerning the word of life—this life was revealed, and we have seen it and testify to it, and declare to you the eternal life that was with the Father and was revealed to us—we declare to you what we have seen and heard so that you also may have fellowship with us; and truly our fellowship is with the Father and with his Son Jesus Christ. We are writing these things so that our joy may be complete [1 John 1:1–4].

The perichoretic fellowship of God is not selfish. It reaches out to us and embraces us and draws us in. Rublev drew these symbols as a way of demonstrating the many ways in history that God has worked to restore fellowship with us. This fellowship of God is itself culture creating.

Church leaders must fill congregational life with the symbols, music, literature, liturgy, and life of God's fellowship. When we do these things, aided by the Spirit of God, we are creating the culture of the Kingdom.

Workplace Culture Creators

Modern corporate leaders today are learning the importance of creating enduring organizational cultures. Many recent publications reflect the trend toward intentional culture creating to build company loyalty and effectiveness. Church leaders have generally steered clear of business resources when it comes to creating culture. We fear that the corporate culture is entrenched with aggressive and hostile behaviors and structures we would not want to emulate in the church. There are, nonetheless, things we as church leaders can learn from those on the growing edge of creating business cultures. Although the visions and methods of church and corporation may differ, some of the tools and understandings used by organizational innovators can help church leaders learn new skills for culture-creating teams. Like the characteristics of the postmodern world, these tools and understandings can be put through a theological grid, and what filters through can be quite helpful for the church today.

Business thinkers Terrence Deal and Allan Kennedy (1982) have studied certain enduring companies and discovered that they all have in common strong corporate cultures. Examining early leaders of U.S. business such as Thomas Watson at IBM, Harley Procter of Procter & Gamble, and General Johnson of Johnson & Johnson, Deal and Kennedy have come to the conclusion that good organizational leadership is characterized by "almost fanatical attention to the culture of their companies." In fact, "a strong culture has almost always been the driving force behind continuing success in American business" (p. 5).

A strong culture is not necessarily a *good* culture, but Deal and Kennedy argue that many strong, enduring companies have tried to incorporate good ethics and core values as part of their corporate structures. William Cooper Procter of Procter & Gamble, for example, told his successor, Richard Deupree, "Always try to do what's right. If you do that, nobody can really find fault" (p. 27). Interestingly, William Procter's cousin, Harley Procter, came up with the name of one company product—Ivory Soap—in church, while reciting verse 8 of Psalm 45: "All thy garments smell of myrrh and aloe, and cassia, out of the ivory palaces whereby they have made thee glad" (p. 26).

Some of the strongest corporate cultures have also made people a high priority in a manner that reflects what Christians believe about the worth and dignity of human beings. Deal and Kennedy note that Tandem showed its employees a lot of respect and worked to cultivate a corporate culture of respect. One of the understandings that formed a core value at Tandem was that all its people, "managers, vice-presidents, and even janitors, communicate on the same level. No one feels better than anyone else" (p. 10).

A strong, respectful corporate culture also creates what we in the church call fellowship. Tandem was known for its ritual of Friday afternoon parties attended by all employees. The event was more than a friendly way to celebrate a week's work; it served to create informal networks of communication and mingling across employee lines. A company like Tandem would be more likely to have a cross section of society represented at one of these Friday afternoon parties than would any given church on Sunday morning.

James Collins and Jerry Porras (1994) also studied enduring—what they called *visionary*—companies. Although they would agree that an enduring company is not necessarily a *good* company in terms of spiritual values, they too argue for the importance of culture creating as a way of building strong, lasting organizations. Observing IBM, they note that founder Thomas Watson plastered the walls of the young, struggling company with slogans that would evolve into IBM's legendary core values. He started training programs to systematically indoctrinate new employees into the corporate culture, intentionally sought to hire young and impressionable people, instituted strict rules of personal conduct, established a required dress code, and "sought to create a heroic mythology about employees who best exemplified the corporate ideology" (p. 125). In its early days IBM even had an IBM songbook, which included the company's own anthem (p. 125):

> March on with I.B.M.
>   Work hand in hand,
> Stout hearted men go forth,
>   In every land.

Another good example of building corporate culture that can be educational for church leaders can be found in the Disney Corporation and its remarkable success in the theme park industry. When Disney World uses holographs and hidden speakers to create "magical" effects, it is fooling us. Those ghosts in the Haunted House are actually clever projections. But what *is* real is Disney's legendary ability to create a culture that *guests* (as Disney calls visitors to its parks) find appealing and, well, magical. Behind the fun and smiles is the serious business of culture creating.

Tom Connellan (1996) describes a special walking tour, led by then Disney *cast member* (employee) Mort Vandeleur, to show several people the seven keys to Disney's success. While Mort and the tour members munched on an early breakfast near the Magic Kingdom's City Hall, Mort saw a family looking confused as they tried to make out a Disney map.

> Excusing himself from the group, he went outside and began talking with the family. At one point, he bent down and said something to one of the children. The little girl, who appeared to be about ten years old, broke out in a big smile. Mort pointed . . . and the family looked off in the direction indicated, nodded, and seemed grateful for his help.
>
> "What was going on there?" [someone in the tour group asked] . . . when Mort returned.
>
> "What I was just doing was being 'aggressively friendly,'" Mort explained. "All cast members are strongly urged to stop whatever they're doing, if they can, and offer help whenever they see a guest in need. . . . If they see guests puzzling over a map, they offer help. If someone's trying to take a group photo, they offer to take the picture

so everyone can be in the shot. As you come in on the monorail, the announcer says, 'You're about to arrive at the most magical place in the world.' Every cast member wants to preserve that magical experience. Every one of them wants to help guests enjoy their visit to the fullest extent possible. They don't just talk about it. That would be 'talking the talk.' They do it. That's 'walking the talk.' Guests will average sixty contact opportunities—points where they come in contact with a cast member. Disney wants to make each of those a magic moment. Cast members actively seek out the opportunity to create one of those magic moments" [pp. 40–41].

That's culture creating. And at Disney it is not make-believe. Seventy percent of Disneyland's business is from return customers. Even though its prices are among the highest in the industry, people come back because the culture is so inviting and appealing. Michael Eisner, Disney's CEO, would be the first to tell us, though, that creating culture begins at the top. Unless the top executives are living the culture, it does not happen. Walking the talk applies to them even more than to any of the other cast members. "Yesterday [said Vandeleur] we saw Michael [Eisner] pick up a piece of paper and toss it into a trash can. Every time that happens—which is anytime Michael sees trash in the park—that says more about the importance of cleanliness than any policy or procedure that could ever be written" (Connellan, 1996, p. 47). Eisner responded to Vandeleur by saying, "But just as important, probably more so, is the fact that every supervisor does the same thing. Dick Nunis, chairman of Walt Disney Attractions, and Judson Green, president of Walt Disney Attractions, pick up litter along with everybody else. So this commitment to cleanliness is ingrained in everyone's mindset" (p. 47).

Disney demonstrates a key leadership quality that is helpful for church leaders to learn. Culture creating works only if those with the most responsibility for leadership walk the talk. Effective organizations are led by individuals or teams that live the dream. I have heard cable television and social entrepreneur Bob Buford (author of *Halftime,* 1997) say many times, "The effective social entrepreneur is the one willing to sleep on the floor for the project."

The IBM anthem that sounds more religious than corporate and the emphasis at Disney on walking the talk are just two illustrations of the fact that some of the trends and practices of postmodern culture—and specifically, in this case, corporate culture—are actually important characteristics of *any* effective organization. Yet in making use of the *particular* cultural trends I am describing (by no means *all* cultural trends), the church is not imitating the corporate world so much as *rediscovering* that which was once central to Christian faith. As I have been emphasizing, these cultural trends give the church the opportunity to learn how to build solid, enduring *Christian* organizations that exhibit the perichoretic fellowship of God in the world.

Building Culture-Creating Teams

The culture of the principal leadership team has an enormous effect on the congregational culture and even the community at large. The best way for this leadership team to influence the church and the town environments is to exhibit and live the vision and mission of the church. The lived culture becomes contagious and is replicated in various ways throughout the church and community, both intentionally and unconsciously. Over time the culture is exported by individual church leaders out into their various arenas of ministry.

A comment I heard at a Bible study illustrates the kind of effect a strong church culture lived by the leaders can have on an individual. Reverend Constance Jordan-Haas, who serves on the pastoral team at Noroton Presbyterian Church in Darien, Connecticut, has led this study for years, and the participants' fellowship has created a strong culture all its own. During one meeting, a woman complimented Jordan-Haas on her leadership style, particularly her listening skills. "Connie, you listen so well!" she exclaimed. "I have noticed that since I've been a member of this Bible study. Because of your style, I am a better Junior High School teacher. I listen better to my students. This is a skill I learned from you, Connie. By watching you lead us, I've become a better teacher!" Do not underestimate the impact of good leadership teams. Their example and their influence are enormous!

The following are ways a team can build a culture that, in turn, has considerable effects on the congregation at large and reaches even beyond those in the pews.

Eliminate Competing Cultures

In some cases, pastors make the mistake of thinking the staff environment is the *least* important place to begin developing a nurturing congregational culture. After all, they reason, the staff team is *paid*. We don't have to treat them like volunteers. We can hold them to a job description and make them do their jobs. The other ministry teams in the church are volunteers. Therefore, this reasoning goes, the staff can be treated like hired hands whereas the volunteers need to be treated differently. In fact, some think it is better not to get too relational with staff because we never know when we might have to terminate a staff person's employment.

Two competing cultures, then, can emerge in a church: one that nurtures and supports a kinder, friendlier environment for volunteers and another that supports a hard-nosed employment environment governed by a strict personnel handbook and stern supervisors.

The concept that we can treat hired hands differently from volunteers because we can threaten their paychecks is not only obsolete in the postmodern world but, frankly, un-Christian. The best workers, be they paid or unpaid, work not for money but to embark on a sacred quest. Remember, it is the vision that unites and inspires, not the pastor's personal charisma or the paycheck. Church employees who work because they are threatened rather than out of love and devotion to Christ and God's mission for that congregation will not give good service to the church.

Create one culture that combines the best parts of the way volunteers are treated and the way staff are treated. Treat staff and volunteers as people who have enlisted for a vital Christian cause. View staff not as slaves who must reinforce the Christian culture *or else,* but as dedicated leaders whom the church has chosen to guide and lead it in its specific mission. Cultivate a culture that treats the paid staff with the same respect, support, and encouragement as that given to the volunteer leaders. Evaluate paid staff not as individuals isolated from the volunteer leaders of the church but rather as those intimately engaged with the congregation in living out their particular area of the total vision for the church. Make sure the same core values of care, compassion, forgiveness, and exhortation extended to the whole congregation are also lived out among the principal leadership team. If they are not, the congregation will perceive it as hypocritical. Jesus modeled with the twelve apostles the kind of fellowship they were to emulate around the Roman world. So should church leaders.

Model the Character of the Group

I have mentioned before the importance of the pastor or other primary leader in building effective, meaningful church ministry teams. Without this leader's commitment, the ministry will fail. This is especially true when it comes to culture building. This leader models to the principal leadership team the qualities of the desired culture for the congregation.

For example, Buford Karraker works hard to build a relational staff culture that will, in turn, influence his congregation, Northwest Church in Fresno, California. During his thirty years of ministry to this church, the congregation has grown from seventy-five people meeting in a little chapel to a worship attendance of over two thousand.

Northwest Church is known in Fresno as a highly relational, caring church. The congregation has had a significant impact in Fresno and beyond through providing not only Christian services but ministry to community needs such as programs for youths at risk. The strong, caring nature of the church's influence starts with the leadership team. Karraker described to me how he makes it a point to model the important values of the church with his staff: "It all begins with an annual retreat. We load up all twenty-four of the principal staff and go off to a big cabin in the mountains. We live together, eat together, clean together and really get to know and care about each other. This retreat of care and concern sets the mood for the rest of the year."

The theme of care and concern for one another and for each person's ministry is then carried out through regular staff meetings. "At those staff meetings every other week," Karraker explained, "we pile into my office. It's tight, but it's the atmosphere I want to create. We met for a while in one of those conference rooms, but it was cold and sterile. In my office, we're cozy. I go through their reports and talk about the various things we need to be caring and praying about."

Northwest Church works to cultivate an environment that communicates that the church really cares about people. "They won't get one of those dang automated answering machines here at Northwest," said Karraker. "We tell folks in every way that we care about them and what they're experiencing. We're not going to give them some electronic voice that tells them to push buttons for staff. We're going to answer the phone with a real person who cares about them." That real person, in turn, experiences the care of the staff team. The culture is contagious!

Karraker models what he wants his staff and congregation to be and do in other ways. He creates the culture he wants perpetuated. "During the hymns, I walk out in the congregation and touch folks and talk to them. I want them to know we care." On one occasion, he intuited that one of his staff was going through a difficult time so he asked another staff member to scout out the problem. In this way, says Karraker, he encouraged one staff member to care for another. He put that staff member in a position to carry out the culture. Isn't this what Jesus did with his disciples?

Make Heroes and Heroines

An important element in the culture of any group is storytelling about its heroes and heroines. Heroic figures model for us what we are called to be and do. They show practical ways for us to live out the mission of the church. The medieval Roman Catholic Church depicted the lives of canonized saints as a way of recognizing *saintly* behavior worthy of imitation. Although Protestant Christians object to lifting one Christian up above another in a heavenly hierarchy (we are all saints of God), the practice of telling saintly stories is quite helpful in any church. The hero is not made out to be greater than life or better than everyone else. Rather, the story of the church hero simply tells how God used him or her to live out a part in the church's mission. Not only should the hero not be greater than most in the congregation, it is better that he or she be perceived as like everyone else, so that the prospect of living for Christ in the world is not thought of as only for the especially gifted, the elite, or the well-to-do.

Rick Warren at Saddleback Church in southern California will pull a hero right out of the congregation as he preaches (it's prearranged). The person's story fits the sermon and he or she becomes a living demonstration of the point Warren is making.

Use Existing Culture as a Springboard for Change

Ministry teams are most effective when they create new church cultures by building the new on the base of the old, on the congregation's existing traditions, symbols, language, and history. Leaders of new churches need to be aware only of the culture of the region to create the church culture that best ministers to the local population. They are like missionaries, using the local language and worldview to communicate the Gospel. But most church leaders find themselves part of existing congregations. They are not in a position to start a new worshiping congregation from zero. They must be not only aware of the culture of the region but also sensitive to the congregation's existing unique traditions as they create a new culture that supports the new, sharper vision.

Jeff Crosno of First Church of the Nazarene in Portland, Oregon, approached his new pastorate with an understanding of cultural dynamics in the existing congregation. This is the church of the founder of the Nazarene denomination. It is steeped in history and heritage. Crosno knew that change was needed but also that the culture of the existing church was deeply embedded. So he decided to learn everything he could learn about the history of the church. He listened intently to the many stories that made up the living memory of the church's significant moments, accomplishments, and failures. Over time, he became the best teller of the church's story. He said to me, "not only did I tell the stories of the church that they knew, but people learned new stories they had never heard before. I became the keeper of the church's stories built into one overarching story."

With this understanding of his church, Crosno initiated change with his leadership team that naturally flowed out of the church's identity. Both he and the members of the leadership team felt that God was calling them to build upon the parts of the cultural foundation that were good and strong. From that foundation grew a new, visionary culture.

Crosno's approach shows a lot of wisdom. Pastors and other church leaders sometimes try to import ideas alien to a church's culture. These ideas might have worked for a pastor in a different church, but they have no cultural antecedent in the present church to build on. Just as God used the history of Israel to demonstrate God's faithfulness and promises—a history that was punctuated with significant, memorable events that became a story of redemption and hope—so God has been at work in churches, and their existing cultures reflect some of God's leading. Leadership teams must work to identify the strong good points of a congregation's culture and build on them, as the Spirit leads and enables, to create new and renewing church cultures.

Use Language, Liturgy, Symbols, History, Traditions, Customs, and Slogans

Effective ministry teams need to be immersed in the culture they want the congregation to emulate. Employing those things we associate with a congregational culture, we can create an ethos, founded on the congregation's existing traditions, that reinforces the purpose God has given to our church. Leadership teams use language, liturgy, symbols, history, traditions, customs, and slogans in creating this culture.

First Church of Appleton can exemplify how a leadership team can use language, liturgy, and similar tools in creating culture for itself and for the whole congregation. Recall the vision statement for First Church:

> First Church of Appleton is committed to
> - *Worship,* that both feeds the believer and appeals to the unbeliever

- *Nurture,* that draws people into a closer discipleship with Jesus Christ
- *Mission,* that is enabled by the release of the spiritual gifts of its members

The leadership team and elder board agreed that the worship goal would be met through two worship services, one designed for the believer on Sunday morning and one designed for the unbeliever (that is, seeker oriented) on Saturday evening. The nurture goal could be achieved through a variety of small-group studies and activities with a clear design of taking people deeper in their knowledge and understanding of the faith. The mission goal could be accomplished through a gifts assessment program and a coordinating team that would connect each person's gift with a ministry or mission need.

After the process of determining the church's vision and planning specifically how the leadership would begin to implement the vision, the leadership team turned to creating a culture that reenforced the vision. First Church staff worked to create a visual illustration of their three-prong vision: worship, nurture, mission. The town symbol in Appleton was a distinctive apple tree that was characteristic of the area and grown for commercial purposes. First Church leadership drew an image of that same tree, emboldening the central part of the trunk and branches to form a cross. The upper branches of the tree were redrawn slightly to resemble uplifted hands in worship. Two birds were drawn in those higher branches in a symbolic reference to Psalm 84, verses 1 to 4. The word *worship,* in small letters, was placed at the top of the tree near those branches. On the left side of the tree were drawn adults and children, male and female, reaching up and eating from the fruit of the tree. Here was the word *nurture.* On the right side of the tree were a man and a woman reaching up for the apples with one hand and reaching out in a giving gesture with the other hand. In this corner of the picture was the word *mission.* At the bottom of the symbolic drawing were the words, "First Church of Appleton" and underneath that, in smaller scripted letters, "A Vibrant Congregation in Worship, Nurture and Mission!"

As people walked into the church office at First Church of Appleton, their eyes immediately fell on a large drawing of the apple tree symbol above the receptionist's desk. Down both halls were framed representations of "apple core values." The first one, for example, depicted the apple tree symbol of the church and the inscription, "We view each other as brothers and sisters created in the image of God with value and purpose." The second one had the same symbol with the inscription, "We love because Christ first loved us, and we are determined to show forth this love in Appleton." Underneath this inscription were several photographs of houses First Church had built with Habitat for Humanity. Many other such visual displays of apple core values lined the office building hallways.

On the desk of each staff member was an attractive brass apple paperweight with the inscription, "We thank God that you are with us to teach us how to bear the fruit of the Spirit in the world. Your Appleton Church family." A hymn was written and sung frequently by the staff, who then taught it to the congregation, with this first verse and refrain:

> We gather in Worship, Nurture and Mission
> On a Hill of Appleton Way,
> Moved by God's grace and empowering vision,
> Wind of the Spirit blown into clay.
> > *Praise you, Praise you, Almighty God;*
> > *You have loved us as cherished children.*
> > *Praise you, Praise you Almighty God;*
> > *You have loved us as your very own.*

Each staff member had a personalized Apple mug. The red and green colors used to depict the tree symbol of the church were used throughout the offices in artwork, paint, and upholstery. The leadership team reserved a time in its weekly meeting for acknowledging a member of the church for an action that was a good example of bearing the fruit of the Spirit. These heroic stories of faith were shared in worship with the congregation and written about in church publications.

In ways such as these, First Church of Appleton sought to immerse both the staff and the congregation in the culture that supported the church's purpose. This purpose was graphically portrayed in ways that the typical member of the church could quickly grasp God's vision for the congregation and sense how he or she might be a part of it. In a brief fifteen-minute conversation, the pastor was able to share with each new member class the vision of the church, the ways it was practically fulfilling that vision, and it's organizational structure by using various visual aids, images, stories, and sayings that could be found repeated and reinforced throughout the congregation's environment.

Communicate, Communicate, Communicate!

Church leadership must use every communication tool available to acculturate the staff and congregation in the mission of the church. As I have said before, be visual. Appeal to the senses. Make it easy for people to

THE CULTURE-CREATING TEAM

know quickly what it is the congregation is about (even though the actual *living and fulfilling* of that mission are not easy). Make mailings attractive and repeat often the mission of the church and how it is being fulfilled. Lift up individuals who are living the vision and make them heroes and heroines of the congregation. Use the Internet. At the church Web site make audio and video clips available that reinforce the mission. Show pictures of the congregation involved in its central mission enterprises. Use representative colors, and use the congregation's special hymn to provide a musical introduction. The Internet is an excellent and cheap source of communication. In years past, congregations have spent millions of dollars to communicate via television and satellite. The Internet can provide many of these same communication services for a fraction of the cost.

Music, Music, Music!

Ministers sometimes tell revealing jokes: for example, "When Satan fell from heaven, he landed in the middle of the choir loft!"

I am certain directors of church music tell their own jokes about pastors. And pastors tend to agree that ways of thinking, experiencing, and perceiving in the music department are different from those found among the clergy. Sometimes these differences break out into conflict and rebellion. Pastors sometimes react to such situations by trying to minimize the influence and involvement of the music ministry in the life of the congregation. But the opposite is needed. Never before in U.S. church history has collaboration between pastors and musicians been more important.

Pastors and church musicians must forge strong, good working relationships because music is more important to congregations in the postmodern world than it was in the modern world. Because the perception of reality in the postmodern world is highly experiential, music must play a greater role in culture creating and maintaining.

Rick Warren once commented to me that every mass renewal and spiritual awakening in history has been accompanied by a new genre of music. Reformed hymns grew up around the Calvinist movement in sixteenth-century Geneva. The Methodist societies were filled with vibrant new songs written by the Wesley brothers and Fanny Crosby. The new paradigm churches such as the Vineyard Fellowship and Hope Chapel are being accompanied by new expressions of contemporary Christian music. Music must not be undervalued or given a backseat when it comes to creating a specific church ethos. If the music used does not fit the culture desired, the attempt to create a specific environment will be severely hampered. Church leaders need to design music intentionally to reflect the mission and goal of the congregation and the people it seeks to attract.

For decades, Peninsula Bible Church in Palo Alto, California, attracted a remarkably diverse crowd to its Sunday evening Body Life worship services, led by the late Pastor Ray Stedman. A key addition to the strong biblical message was the innovative music led by young Christian musicians, who often came out of the secular musical scene to adapt their contemporary styles for Christian worship. Some of the best in contemporary Christian music has come out of the environment of entrepreneurial churches seeking to reach out to new generations with the life-changing Gospel of Jesus Christ.

Some churches choose to preserve traditional liturgy in some of their worship services but give the music a face-lift. First Presbyterian Church in Colorado Springs is a good example of a church that often uses traditional music but with a flair. The otherwise staid organ is accompanied by a variety of other instruments, giving it a fuller, more encompassing sound. This kind of music tends to satisfy the traditional Presbyterian worshiper while appealing also to those who have not been in church for many years.

Tom Brown, director of music at Covenant Presbyterian Church in Austin, Texas, has been an innovator in creating all jazz worship services. Jazz Sunday is attended by hundreds of people who come to worship Christ with music that comes out of the depths of America's soul. The multiple Sunday morning services are followed by a jambalaya fellowship and jazz concert. How easy it is to use the jazz theme and relate it to the African American experience of slavery in our early history as a nation. The blues and the laments of the Christian hunched over and picking cotton in the hot sun have meaningful contemporary application for the church today.

Some church leaders will feel that their meager music budget is stretched as far as it can go and that they lack the volunteer resources to enlarge their music in worship. These leaders are probably already engaging in prayer, asking God for musical leaders to catch the vision for their churches and assist them. In addition to prayer, church leaders can make music enhancement a mission enterprise and use mission funds to enlarge music in worship for a specified period of time. I suggest that fuller, more meaningful worship services, the kind this book is describing how to create, tend to develop momentum and grow congregations. This is not a guarantee. It may be that in some communities being faithful to the Gospel will make a church's congregation shrink. But, generally speaking, given the spiritual hunger in the United States today, churches that take some risks and create church cultures that are innovative and outreaching, tend to grow and so do their budgets. An investment in enhanced music can result over time in a return of those funds used to launch the program. The mission team could, in effect, be paid back for its worship investment. And if the result of enhanced worship is greater attendance by those who previously did not attend church, then I would suggest it was not just a good music investment but a good mission investment in the first place.

Aim for Some Cultural Diversity

Some will argue that the kind of culture creating I am suggesting results in a congregation that is too homogeneous and forces out people who do not fit the new environment. This criticism is a useful reminder, and leadership teams should be cautious not to create cultures that are too narrow. Some church cultures are intentionally structured to deprive the congregation of balance. For example, a congregation might espouse very strong Republican political views, to the degree that Christians who are Democrats may feel unwelcome. I suggest that defining a church culture in such narrow terms can excessively shelter a congregation from the larger environment and prevent people from developing a balanced way of both perceiving reality and living out Christian ministry.

Having acknowledged the value of this criticism, I suggest that all churches possess a clear culture, whether they are intentional about it or not. A mainline U.S. church in a white suburb may not do any of the things I have suggested to intentionally shape its culture but may still project, in many unconscious and unintentional ways, a strongly white, European-based environment. Look at the cars in the parking lot on Sunday, the neighborhood where the church is located, the dress of the worshiper, the vestments of the clergy, the language and music of the liturgy, the educational level of the sermon, and the topics of discussion in both formal classes and informal meetings around the coffee pot—all these factors and many more indicate a distinct culture that will invite some people and exclude others. I suggest that the churches that are quite intentional about the cultures they create are, paradoxically, far more likely to have a wider appeal (particularly when diversity is a stated core value of their culture) than are the churches that preach a message of diversity but are in practice culturally homogeneous. The sermon spoken by the culture is far louder and carries much more influence than the sermon spoken from the pulpit. If we are willing to put many hours of preparation into our pulpit sermons and worship services then why are we not also willing to be planned and prepared and intentional about the sermons our cultures preach?

Media, Media, Media!

Michael Slaughter, pastor of Ginghamsburg Church in Tipp City, Ohio, has pioneered the use of a remarkable variety of media to communicate the Gospel in worship. His book *Out on the Edge* (1997), which outlines much of the theology, strategy, and practice of his congregation in using media to create church culture, includes a CD, further driving home his point that we live today in a *postliterate,* postmodern world that requires of the church the ability to use media resources to communicate to the unchurched. Slaughter quite persuasively argues that the church, once a leader in communication using the arts, has lagged behind the media revolution and needs to catch up with all the others who are using audiovisual and electronic media to communicate their messages. He wishes to convince us of the importance of using all the media possible to communicate effectively the life-changing Word of God:

> Why is media a life and death issue for the Church? Whoever controls the media controls the values and direction of the postmodern culture: a media-driven culture where children kill children for Michael Jordan gym shoes (valued at $125) and learn their sexual values from "Baywatch." Who will define reality in a virtual-reality world that goes from Barney the purple dinosaur to babies dying in Rwanda at the push of a remote control button? Will sadistic movies like "Pulp Fiction" and "Natural Born Killers" define humor for postmoderns? . . .
>
> Followers of Jesus were given the ability by God to communicate in the contemporary language of the culture. Electronic media are much more than entertainment [p. 63].

Slaughter challenges the church to adopt the communication media of the larger culture and become expert communicators in order to influence society and draw unbelievers to Christ.

Churches around the country are heeding Slaughter's advice. Menlo Park Presbyterian Church in Menlo Park, California, is an example of a congregation using a variety of audiovisual media in worship. A worshiper at one of Menlo Park's five weekend services need never look *down* at a bulletin or hymnbook. The lyrics of hymns and songs are attractively displayed on two large screens, which silently roll out from the walls above the chancel (front of the sanctuary). Scripture readings and other information are displayed there as well, along with visuals that enhance worship and aid communication of the day's theme. Mission presentations during worship services are transformed when the worshiper can see the mission field and work of a particular missionary. Church members comment on being "right there, close and personal" with a baby as it is baptized, because closed-circuit television cameras zoom in on the child and display the Sacrament's action to the congregation on the two large central screens and numerous monitors positioned throughout the sanctuary. Worshipers feel closer to the action of worship. Their singing is louder and uplifted because they are looking up. The visual images and colors enhance the theme and mood of worship.

The church in the postmodern world must learn to use electronic media to communicate because, in Slaughter's words, they are "the language of our culture" (1997, p. 63). But even when an individual church lacks the capability to employ sophisticated technology to communicate, it still has many ways it can use its given resources to be better at culture creating. Centuries-old liturgies can be refreshed and revised with language, symbols, and actions that fit the local context and people's postmodern expectations of church culture. The making of such reforms will be occasions for church renewal that can bring about a dramatic difference in the life and mission of a local congregation.

6

THE COLLABORATIVE TEAM

COLLABORATIVE MINISTRY teams that have a clear purpose and rigorous discipline are a highly effective way of creating spiritually fulfilling work and moving toward a Christ-centered goal. Team ministry has a solid biblical and theological foundation that, in most cases, sets it above Lone Ranger heroics as the most meaningful way to serve in the church. A team that learns how to discern the spiritual gifts of the individual team members and how to have members work together, pray hard, and share information and energy in order to move toward a sharply defined mission, vision, or cause, is an extremely powerful unit of ministry.

When members of leadership teams collaborate in order to accomplish what they discern is God's will, they experience the beauty of Spirit-given synergy. People feel as though they have made important contributions to help move the group toward a meaningful end. In contrast, groups that falter and fizzle out lack a high degree of collaboration. People wind up feeling at best confused about what they were supposed to be doing and frustrated that the group could not work together. At worst, people feel abused and resentful because their freely offered gifts were not used or perhaps were even misused.

Moving Beyond Slogans

First Church of Appleton has made progress. Its ministry leaders and its congregation had been in conflict as a result of fragmentary ministry departments. Then the pastor and the principal leadership team successfully covenanted (Chapter Three) to model Christian fellowship to the congregation and the other leaders. The unity of the leadership team and its insistence on working through its problems for the sake of the church quelled potential rebellion but did not eliminate the structural problems that created competition among ministry centers. The process resulting in a sharper vision (Chapter Four) for the congregation provided the mission around which all the ministries now orbit. Having a clear sense of God's purpose for the congregation, the leadership team has started to create the church culture (Chapter Five) that will reinforce that purpose and direct energy and resources toward accomplishing it. Leaders must now learn how to collaborate as a team (rather than compete as lone religious professionals) to build that culture and move toward ministry goals.

Collaboration is the art and skill of negotiating community, networking gifts, and focusing individual contributions to fit into the larger movement of the faithful fellowship. All the progress that First Church of Appleton has achieved may come to an abrupt halt if collaborative team building is not accomplished. Certainly team covenanting, vision shaping, and culture creating will do much to improve the morale and ministries of the leaders and the congregation. But the actual accomplishment of significant ministry goals will be limited if this skill of collaboration is not learned and mastered. In learning to collaborate we put legs on the theology of the body of Christ and take steps to walk the talk of working together. At this point, First Church's ministry would be little more than slogans and banners if people were not challenged *to do community.*

Building a collaborative team is first the responsibility of the principal leadership team. Team progress in this effort becomes a model and symbol to the other ministry groups in the church. Team learning about collaboration, disseminated throughout the congregation through the normal communication channels, becomes shared wisdom for others to follow. Because collaboration is a difficult skill requiring trial and error, permission is needed to fail at collaboration and to discuss these failures. The failures then serve as teaching tools for the other groups in the church. Grace needs to be extended as team members learn how to work together and keep each other accountable for their progress.

The First Church staff began to learn new things about each other because they were spending more time in honest sharing. For example, they learned that the associate pastor who led the youth ministry was getting tired of doing youth ministry. He was, however, developing a related passion for helping families and marriages stay together. The team affirmed his giftedness in both youth and family ministry. Representatives of the team approached the elder board, discussed what the team had learned, and recommended that the youth pastor hire a youth team to work under his direction while he focused on developing a new ministry for family and marriage enrichment. The youth pastor continued to have gifts for youth ministry that he could use to teach and develop a new youth leadership team. Moving his primary work into the new area of service to marriages and families released a new energy in him.

"To be honest," he reported to the leadership team, "I was beginning to circulate my résumé. Now I realize I do not feel called to leave First Church. I just needed to change focus and work in an area I care deeply about developing." Team members felt a high degree of satisfaction that they had helped a fellow team member clarify his role in ministry and helped him feel more fulfilled. Furthermore, the associate pastor's new enthusiasm resulted in growth that more than funded, through new contributions, the additional youth staff.

The addition of marriage and family ministries and other staff for youth ministries meant that the new youth and family ministries budget grew larger than the music budget. For years, the youth and music budgets had been the same. This time around, however, the music director had been involved in the team process of discerning each team member's gifts and passions for ministry. He had heard the youth pastor share his frustrations about ministry. Both these leaders were part of a larger team process, working to discern what they could do *as a team* to benefit their congregation and community. The music director explained to his main sanctuary choir, "I am excited about this change for the youth pastor. You ought to have seen him after the board approved the new family ministry. He was ecstatic! And, you know, having been with the church for six years now, I know firsthand how badly we need family and marriage enrichment. I am excited about this new development, even if it means we have to wait another year to get some of the new things we want. Besides, the new family and marriage enrichment programs are drawing in new members, some of whom want to serve the church in music ministries. We got a trumpet player through the new programs."

The leaders of First Church of Appleton are making progress toward significant ministry goals by collaborating. As important (some would say more important) as moving toward these task accomplishments is the good feeling generated when team members work together. This good feeling created by collaborative teamwork is accompanied by a sense that the work has ultimate meaning. Morale at First Church has improved, and team members feel as though their contributions are indispensable to the group. The good will created by collaboration reverberates throughout the whole congregation and results in a more team-oriented, collaborative congregation. Indeed, members even take the skills of community building learned in the church and live them out in their homes and offices. The potential influence of First Church for more meaningful relationships in the town of Appleton is enormous.

Team Play

I learned the advantages of collaborative teamwork many years ago, serving as an assistant coach for my son's soccer team. Recruited by the head coach, I was given the job of working on basic skills with the elementary school kids. Over a year, the coach and I saw a remarkable transformation. In the early games the players looked like a swarm of bees chasing after the ball. No one stayed in position; they all just chased after the ball in a big mob. But over time we taught collaboration and teamwork. Beginning with basic skills, we worked to discern the individual talents and gifts of the children. A kid with good dribbling and passing skills ended up as a halfback. Accurate shooters became forwards. A kid with a strong left foot found his element as left wing. Some of our stout, hard-to-knock-over kids became fullbacks. One particularly quick and agile kid became goalie. We emphasized the need to stay in position, control the ball, and then pass it forward. The second half of the season was significantly more successful than the first as the children worked together, contributing their unique talents in their specific positions, to accomplish goals for the team. As coaches, we found satisfaction not so much in winning or losing, but in seeing good plays executed by kids working together. We also observed that the teams we played that had an exceptional player or two tended to depend heavily on their stars whereas the rest of their game was sloppy. Our team had no superstar. Instead, we learned to play with order and cohesion—and became tough to beat!

Teams are made up of people who are diverse in skill and temperament. Each member contributes skill and knowledge for the benefit of the group's goal. This collaboration is synergistic, producing a net effect that far outweighs the sum of the work of individuals. The leaders at First Church of Appleton must now learn to work together as a collaborative team to lead the congregation in pursuit of its divine mission.

The Body of Christ as Team Ministry

The church has known the power of God working through collaborative groups long before the postmodern management and business world discovered the power of even secular teamwork. Yet, like other leadership concepts discussed in this book, we let it slip away. We exchanged Paul's notion of the church as the body of Christ for a clergy-centered *parish model* of ministry that usurped the role of the laity.

The English and Scottish parish systems are examples of this parish model. A priest or minister is supplied for a geographical area, and this cleric is responsible for the spiritual welfare of his parishioners; they are the recipients of his ministry. Just as a doctor practices medicine and a lawyer practices law so the cleric dispenses religion. After centuries of such hierarchical parish systems, the authority and responsibility that once belonged to the laity was transferred to the priests and pastors; in a system of ministry that no longer reflected the nature of the early church as described in the acts of the Apostles and the writings of Paul.

Paul described a type of team ministry in terms of the human body (1 Cor. 12–14). The church represented as the body of Christ is like the human body: diverse, with many different kinds of parts that yet function interdependently. New Testament professor Richard Hays points out that using the body and the necessary cooperation of its different parts as a metaphor for human community was not uncommon in the ancient world. However, this metaphor was most commonly used in emphasizing the need for slaves to stay in their place. Paul radically reinterprets the analogy to mean that the body of Christ has no part more important than another part. Each is gifted for the common good of the whole team. Each contribution is valued and needed (see Hayes, 1997, p. 213).

William Easum (1995) argues that Paul's body of Christ description of the church is a crucial image for congregations today. The sense of camaraderie, fellowship, interdependence, sharing, and intimacy implied in the image fits the self-understanding of Christians in a postmodern world. The parts of the body are each unique and yet connected, allowing for individual identity that is, nonetheless, a part of a greater fellowship with Christ as the head.

The good team leader learns to discern the various gifts of the team. She works to make these strengths shine as she also works to render team members' weaknesses irrelevant. Information is shared, resources are pooled, the vision is reiterated and pursued, and prayer is essential; for though we can find the loaves and fish, and order the crowd in groups of fifty, only the Lord Jesus can give the living bread.

Perichoretic Collaboration

Richard Hayes also finds a relationship between the body of Christ as described by Paul and the triune nature of God, underscoring the emphasis I would place on the perichoresis of the Trinity as a model for team ministry. Even though Paul did not have a developed doctrine of the Trinity (that doctrine would come hundreds of years later), Hayes points out that Paul "*experienced* God as Trinity" in that he described "the activity of God in the community in three synonymous parallel clauses as the working of the Spirit and of the Lord Jesus and of God" (p. 210). These are the clauses (1 Cor. 12:4–6) as Hayes shows them:

varieties of gifts	but the same Spirit
varieties of services	but the same Lord
varieties of activities	but the same God, who activates all of them in everyone

The grammatical form is parallelism. The three sources of the ministries and gifts of God's people are the one God. Once again, we see a sense of meaningful community—of team—enabled by God who is expressed in triune fashion. It is implied that meaningful Christian community is that which is gifted by a God who is, in essence, meaningful community. We find our fulfillment not only in being reconciled to God our creator, but also to one another (2 Cor. 5).

A collaborative team is one that shares its resources and gifts in order to move in harmony toward a divine purpose. This sharing and movement imitate the persons of God in holy fellowship. There is a holy collaboration of the persons of God within God. Three Persons, distinct and yet one, form the nature of the one God revealed to us as Father, Son, and Spirit. These three persons of God are not static but in movement. There is, in God's very self, a dynamic flow of love and of sharing. Henri Nouwen (1987) observed this movement as he studied Rublev's Trinity icon: "The movement from the Father toward the Son and the movement of both Son and Spirit toward the Father become a movement in which the one who prays [the person beholding the icon] is lifted up and held secure" (pp. 20–21). Remember that perichoresis means literally *circle dance*. Dancing requires harmony, shifting together, a kind of give and take in dynamic flow. This movement is a kind of collaboration, a sharing and giving, in purposeful rhythm.

The persons of God in collaborative movement are also found in the Gospel of John: "In the beginning was the Word, and the Word was with God, and the Word was God. He was in the beginning with God. All things came into being through him, and without him not one thing came into being. What has come into being in him was life, and the life was the light of all people. The light shines in the darkness, and the darkness did not overcome it" (John 1:1–5).

The Greek word for *with* in the phrase "and the Word was with God" is *pros*. *Pros* is an active word that indicates movement rather than a sedate *withness*. *Pros* is often translated *toward*. The sense of the passage is, "and the Word was in movement toward God."

The Holy Spirit also is part of this perichoretic movement of God. The Spirit moves between the fellowship of God and the fellowship of believers, forming a communication link. In John's Gospel there is a constant movement by the Spirit between the persons of God and the persons of faith. Through the Spirit, we are drawn up into the holy dance of God: "When the Spirit of truth comes, he will guide you into all the truth; for he will not speak on his own, but will speak whatever he hears, and he will declare to you the things that are to come" (John 16:13).

These Bible verses connote movement, sharing, relating, and communicating. The holy fellowship of God is for us a model of collaboration. Even though we do not know how these three persons of the one God are organically related, and though much of who the Trinity is lies shrouded in mystery, we find in Scripture that God is revealed to us in Father, Son, and Spirit and this revelation is depicted in loving word pictures of fellowship, movement, and intimacy.

Workplace Collaborative Teams

Organizations and businesses in our postmodern culture are caught up in the trend of forming collaborative teams for effective work and service. Teams work best in an environment that values the importance of individual contributions to group efforts, has a flatter (less hierarchical) organizational structure, gives power and permission to smaller groups to accomplish greater tasks (self-managing teams), and satisfies the need of workers to be more actively involved in outcomes.

The Wisdom of Teams, by Jon Katzenbach and Douglas Smith (1994), is an example of recent works published about forming collaborative work groups. The authors believe that such teams can be one of the most efficient and effective ways to accomplish tasks. "We believe that teams—real teams, and not just groups that management calls 'teams'—should be the basic unit of performance for most organizations, regardless of size," they declare. Teams have the potential to deliver the most effect for the energy applied. And "teams are more productive than groups that have no clear performance objectives, because their members are committed to deliver tangible performance results. Teams and performance are an unbeatable combination" (p. 15).

Katzenbach and Smith do not believe that organizing work groups and calling them teams results in real teams. In fact, they observe that many teams in the business world are called teams but are not. These authors define *real teams* in terms that are consistent with the characteristics I have used to describe collaborative teams. They state that "a team is a small number of people with complementary skills who are committed to a common purpose, performance goals, and approach for which they hold themselves mutually accountable (p. 45).

Real teams, then, are small groups that have a sharp mission, collaborate by combining their skills, gifts, and resources to move toward a meaningful (these authors would say *measurable*) goal. They hold one another accountable for the team's progress; an important element of groups that I will bring up again later.

Katzenbach and Smith deliver practical advice for building and maintaining organizational teams. They emphasize the need for discipline in "team basics" to achieve demanding "performance goals." "Team basics include size, purpose, goals, skills, approach, and accountability. Paying rigorous attention to these is what creates the conditions necessary for team performance" (p. 3). And they tell their secular audience, businesses and organizations interested in performance results, that teams work best when "a common, meaningful purpose sets the tone and aspiration" (p. 49). For Christians, what more meaningful purpose is there but to serve the will of God?

Other nationally recognized authors have written on the importance of collaborative leadership and teams. For example, Max De Pree, chairman emeritus of Herman Miller, Inc., and author of several books including *Leadership Jazz,* has spent years wondering how good leaders lead collaborative groups. He thinks of an effective organization as a jazz band. "Jazz-band leaders must choose the music, find the right musicians, and perform—in public. But the effect of the performance depends on so many things—the environment, the volunteers playing in the band, the need for everybody to perform as individuals and as a group, the absolute dependence of the leader on the members of the band, the need of the leader for the followers to play well. What a summary of an organization!" (1992, pp. 8–9).

Leadership jazz! Each instrumentalist contributing, collaborating with the other players, to produce music. A beautiful picture of an organization indeed.

Leaders of collaborative teams know to whom they are indebted. They cannot take all the credit, as Bill Flanagan knows. This vice president of operations for Amdahl Corporation was asked by James Kouzes and Barry Posner (1996) to describe his "personal best" leadership achievement: "After a few moments, Flanagan said that he couldn't do it. Startled, we asked him why. Flanagan replied, 'Because it wasn't *my* personal best. It was *our* personal best. It wasn't *me*. It was *us*.' Leadership is not a solo act. In the thousands of personal-best leadership cases we have studied, we have yet to encounter a single example of extraordinary achievement that occurred without the active involvement and support of many people. We don't expect to find any in the future, either" (p. 106).

Teams with a cause collaborate together to get the job done. The real fun is pursuing the goal and depending on each other. The rewards are in the achievement of the goal much more than in a paycheck. Southwest Airlines won an award at the end of 1997 as one of the best companies to work for as rated by employees of major companies. Southwest's principal leaders have been visionaries who worked hard from the very beginning to create a team culture. Kevin Freiberg and Jackie Freiberg (1996) describe Southwest's shaky beginnings, endured by a team of people who were focused and collaborative:

> The beginning of the first year was tough. Resources were scarce and load factors were very low. Sherry Phelps remembers how rough it was: "We actually bought fuel for a couple of months using Lamar's [then CEO Lamar Muse] personal credit card." The company didn't have a lot of ground equipment either, and what it did have was mostly old and dilapidated. Occasionally, employees found used or abandoned equipment to refurbish. "All of our maintenance was done at night," Jack Vidal, former vice president of maintenance, told us. "Of course, early on we didn't have all the parts we needed, so we'd have to scrounge around. Our people would get on the phone and call friends who worked at Braniff and they'd actually loan us parts" [p. 42].

Southwest's leadership did not hire employees; it hired team players who bought into the leaders' vision. The rewards were camaraderie, friendship, pursuing a meaningful vision, and maybe, a financial payoff if the company were successful.

> "I couldn't understand when I first got there why we didn't have any complaints. Everyone was having a good time," says Howard Putnam. "The employment group worked with the mentality that we hire people who have fun. When I spoke to new employees I'd tell them, 'You've chosen Southwest Airlines and you're going to work harder than at any other airline. You're going to get paid about 30 percent less, but in the long run, when we make this thing work, with your profit-sharing you'll be far ahead of anybody else.' And they are! It is one of the best examples of teamwork I've ever seen" [p. 42].

Here is my question to those of us in the church. If people will work that hard for a scrappy new airline with the promise that maybe, if they work hard and are lucky, they might get ahead financially (actually, I think they did it more for the fun and the challenge than for the money), *then why can't we do as well or better at teamwork for the Savior of the world?*

Building Collaborative Ministry Teams

The first step in building a collaborative team is to ensure that the purpose of the team is clearly defined and generates enthusiasm. There should be a sense that the team's purpose is God given and God directed. (A review of the material about the visionary team [Chapter Four] may be helpful here).

Building a collaborative leadership team is a critical pursuit for churches that desire to go beyond words and church maintenance in order to focus on a specific, God-given mission. *Church maintenance* describes the routine functions of what I have called a generic church, that is, the basic or common church. The generic or routine activities that all churches have in common are essential to the life and faith of the congregation, and I do not intend to minimize the importance of such regular duties as preaching the word and visiting the sick. Collaborative teams work best, however, in an environment that ascribes the regular activities and programs of the church to an overall specific mission. For example, a generic church might be satisfied in listing this item as one of the important activities of the congregation:

> To visit the sick and those in need of healing.

This is a good and noble thing for Christians to be doing. But notice the difference between this activity and the activity put forth by a congregation whose overall emphasis is developing the ministry of the laity:

> To equip and enable the people of the church to visit the sick and those in need of healing so that those in need, having experienced the life-changing power of the Holy Spirit in their lives, might grow in their own faith and discipleship and become themselves those who visit the sick and those in need of healing.

The latter is more specific and more likely to inspire enlistment. Not only are the sick being visited, but there is the added benefit of Christian growth in faith and discipleship for both the visitors and the ones being visited. Furthermore, the statement (which might be used as the purpose statement for a church healing team) fits into the larger church vision of enabling all church members to become disciples of the living Lord and to be equipped for a specific ministry.

Leadership teams should review the vision of their church. Is it sharp enough? Does the leadership team have a clear sense of where it is going and why?

Discover Gifts and Match Them with Passions

The building of effective teams for the long run has to take into account more than gifts and skills. The mistake many of us in leadership make is in forming teams without taking into account individual team members' callings and burdens. How does each individual's burden relate to and inform what a team is all about? The more that team life connects their gifts and skills to the arena of their God-given burden, the more likely you are to have built an effective team for the long haul.

After many years of building teams, Carol Davis at Los Angeles-based LeafLine Initiatives (formerly with The Church on Brady in East Los Angeles) has discovered that gift-based ministry is not enough.

> After several years of building teams with varied degrees of success, I began to realize that the dream and convictions had to be alive in each person's heart, not just in mine. I was calling them to my dream and my burdens . . . not finding out what their dreams were about. They were trying to minister in their gifts area, but that wasn't enough to keep them deeply fulfilled or to sustain the team when the going got rough. Ephesians 4:11–12 convinced me that it was no longer about them being team members for my work of ministry, but about me equipping them for their work of ministry, including finding a place for their unique contributions out of their burdens . . . by way of their gifts and skills.
>
> One of the difficulties is that many have never thought through their own burdens. We began to listen to people's hearts to find the unique things they cared about. Out of their own backgrounds God had crafted and instilled His calling and burdens, even if they were not yet articulated. You only find those by listening to their stories.
>
> For example, we brought into our youth ministry a young adult who had tremendous logistic and administrative gifts. She did what she committed to but always seemed to be holding back. In an infor-

mal conversation, I learned that she had great compassion for abused children. It was in meeting the special needs in children's ministry that she flourished and found her long-term team niche. Just gift-based ministry is not enough when building collaborative teams. You have to tap into the real burden . . . what drives them . . . what they will stay up nights for.

Gifts and skills are the 'how' one ministers. They even help determine team role. The burdens are the 'what,' the 'why,' and the 'where' you minister. They even determine which team you are a part of and long term contributions. When you wrap together God-given burdens and gifts and skills with a team that has a transforming vision, you get personal passion and a powerful long-term team!

Share a Common Philosophy of Ministry

A church team cannot function well when all the members do not subscribe to the same philosophy of ministry. This is one of the most serious problems teams face and one of the most difficult and painful truths I have learned. As with much of my learning, it came out of trial and error. I once thought that church staff members would be on the same key with one another and work in relative harmony if they covenanted together, had a uniting vision, and were dedicated to trusting and supporting one another in a collegial style of ministry. Surely, I thought, these fine characteristics would be strong enough to hold a faithful staff together. I did not yet know how important it is that the team share the same philosophy of ministry. The staff members with whom I have had the most conflicts over the years were not those who differed with me substantially in theology but those who had a different philosophy of ministry. (A philosophy of ministry describes the manner in which ministry ought to be carried out and should be closely related to the culture of the congregation.) I was viewed by these critics as one who was using the wrong methods to accomplish a commonly held purpose. Without agreement on the methods, the staff and I were paralyzed.

For example, I have had fellow team members disagree with me on practical philosophy of ministry issues such as the appropriate style of Christian worship and preaching, the degree to which team leaders (elder committee chairs) should be trusted with spending their allotted budgets, and the ways such basic things as prayer and Bible study should be taught. Even when there is theological agreement about the nature of these enterprises, how they actually get accomplished is a more philosophical matter that can produce conflict.

Staff members can be Christians who agree to abide by a covenant and in every other way seem dedicated to team-based ministry and yet end up fragmented, angry, and weary *if they do not agree on the philosophy of ministry.* I believe team members can be diverse theologically and temperamentally and still work well together if they agree upon a common strategy for doing ministry. But if they differ on this point, collaborative ministry can be stopped in its tracks. It is that important.

Near the beginning of this book I referred to a pastor who had a seeker style of leading worship. His philosophy of ministry was that the church needed to create a culture to reach out to those not attracted to traditional worship. He preached without notes in an informal style, avoided church language that newcomers would not know, and had the director of music use contemporary music. The service reflected the pastor's commitment to outreach.

The associate minister in that same church objected to the pastor's style. He believed that the pastor had forsaken the denominational standards of appropriate worship. The sermon should be preached from the pulpit, proper vestments should be worn, traditional liturgy should be followed as it appeared in the denomination's worship manual, and music should be dignified and traditional. Though committed to the congregation's vision to reach out to new people, he felt convinced that new people should experience traditional worship. Only then could they make a decision about whether or not to become part of that worshiping community.

Once a month, when the associate pastor preached, he made sure the service was changed back into the older style. The pastor fumed, he complained to the worship committee, which found itself divided between the two pastors. The worship committee appealed to the elder board, which was also divided. After tearful, angry congregational forums, in which everyone was allowed to vent feelings, the bishop transferred the associate pastor to another church.

The members of the leadership team at this church did not agree on *how* ministry should be carried out. They knew *why* it should be carried out. They even knew *what* they were called to do (that is, they had a vision). They disagreed on *how* to do it. We sometimes assumed that if we get the *why* and *what* figured out, the *how* will easily follow. It doesn't. It is essential for teams to agree on how to carry out ministry if team members are to work collaboratively. In the previous example, the worship environment cultivated by the pastor differed considerably from the environment created by the associate pastor. This difference became a battle line.

Collaborative leadership teams must determine the philosophy of ministry that will carry out the vision. The church culture will reflect that philosophy, so its design must be intentional and thought through. Leadership teams then must talk about style, custom, language, appearance (for example, vestments), and even symbols. Although individuals' styles of ministry will necessarily differ somewhat, a collaborative strategy for ministry must be forged to avoid the kind of conflict that emerged in the church with conflicting worship environments.

Of course it is possible for a church to have different worship styles supported by a common ministry philosophy. The church that splintered did so because the leadership team did not agree on a common worship style for a particular service. However, many churches successfully conduct multiple worship services, or experiences, that vary considerably. They are able to do this because *the leadership team agrees on how to do it.* In these successful churches, the leader of the contemporary service does not ridicule the leader of the traditional service. Instead, each is supportive of the other's different style and orientation to worship. And each sees the other as accomplishing a different part of the same vision. Their commonly held philosophy of ministry is broad enough to include both styles of worship.

When I recently moved from Austin, Texas, to pastor Noroton Presbyterian Church in Darien, Connecticut, I was surprised at first that this northeastern congregation had not broken apart months before I arrived. Although the church was very ably led by pastors in the past, the years just before I arrived had been marked with considerable trauma through transitions and changes of interim senior pastors. Organizationally, moreover, the church was set up to fail, with separate ministry centers. But the church instead held together remarkably and even grew during a difficult transition. "How did this happen?" I wondered. After a few weeks on the job, I learned the secret of its success. The leaders, both staff and elders, had strong faith, a deep love for one another, and a significant cohesion around a common philosophy of ministry. Although the vision was not strongly stated and no *written* covenant was in place, the church held together, in spite of organizational forces that could have drawn it apart, because of the leaders' collaborative harmony in working together under a common philosophy of ministry.

Ken Baugh agrees. He is the team leader for Frontline, the Generation X ministry at McLean Bible Church in McLean, Virginia. "Our greatest challenge," he told me, "is keeping the leadership together in harmony. I keep everyone talking. Communication is important. We try to maintain a high level of cohesion at the top . . . ah . . . or bottom . . . however you want to call it. If we can't resolve our conflict, how can we expect others in the congregation to resolve conflict?"

McLean has "lots of conflict," but people can "work it out . . . because it has to do with temperament or personality issues. The conflict that can't be resolved is not of this sort, but of the philosophical type. . . . You can't change people's values or philosophy. These things are too close to their identity. It gets pretty sacred there, pretty quick."

When I asked Baugh if that meant that "you don't bring anyone into leadership who is not on track with your vision, goals, and culture?" he said, "Exactly! Otherwise, you're courting disaster. You can't build collaborative teams if you don't have agreement on the essentials of ministry philosophy and vision. It just doesn't work."

As one who has struggled with these issues for many years, I say to you: take heed! Listen to Ken Baugh on this point. Build a collaborative team around a common vision and an agreed-upon formula for accomplishing it!

Some church leaders may be wondering at this point what to do when the *current* leadership team has one or more members who do not fit the culture or the philosophy of ministry adhered to by the majority of the group? A strong church culture will tend to repel naturally those who do not fit it. The same is true of a leadership team's philosophy of ministry. If the way of carrying out the vision of the church is firmly in place and agreed upon by the majority of the team, those members who disagree with it will, over time, tend to either conform to the strategy or remove themselves and find a position that better fits their style. I talk more about helping team members understand whether or not they fit a team or congregational culture in the next section.

Build Team Accountability

Many churches still operate according to a model of keeping paid staff accountable that has lost its effectiveness in a postmodern world and, in my judgment, was never a good model in the first place. According to this older model, each staff member on the principal leadership team has a job description that informs the person about his or her duties and obligations. During annual reviews, the pastor and perhaps a member of a personnel committee reviews the job description with the staff member and notes compliance or lack of compliance with the designated duties. The pastor is considered the head of staff, responsible for ongoing, daily supervision of each staff member. However, the complicated nature of church dynamics creates a convoluted political situation in which the pastor might tell a staff member he is performing under par for his position and the staff member, unhappy with the pastor's assessment, might then turn to his popular constituency in the congregation for support. Very quickly, the pastor finds herself in the position of needing to defend her assessment of the staff member's work in order to deal with the anger of the constituency she has vicariously offended by calling the staff member's work inferior. This common scenario can erupt into a conflagration and even a church split, as evidenced in several notable congregations in the last decade when groups of church members broke off under the new leadership of their favorite staff pastors.

The solution to this problem is to build group accountability in teams, particularly the primary leadership team that is made up of staff. Instead of having a one-on-one accountability relationship with the team leader (usually the pastor for the primary leadership team), each team member *(including the pastor)* is accountable to the whole team for his or her work. The roles and jobs, with their specific duties and responsibilities, are known by the whole team, team members report the progress in their areas at each team meeting, and the particular challenges and struggles of team members in their individual ministry areas are prayed for and understood by the entire team, creating an environment where each member is accountable to the group.

In my experience, creating team accountability is considerably more effective in producing a collaborative, cohesive team than the old head of staff model is. On one occasion, many years ago, my leadership team had a team member who was not doing his job well. It became clear over time that he was simply lazy and not focused. I could have pulled him aside and told him so, but I sensed he was resistant to my leadership in general and to do so would have created antagonism. Instead of confronting him privately, I simply encouraged each team member to report his or her activities at each team meeting. The enthusiasm and focused work of the other staff members contrasted with the lesser activities of the team member who was not working well. The other team members wanted to know if he was spiritually healthy, if he was suffering from depression, or what they could do to help him get focused and involved with his strong gifts in pursuing the team goal. Instead of responding to their encouragement and getting on board with the rest of the team, he resigned and went to work in another church.

Group accountability either helps team members not pulling their weight to get on board and unite with the team or results in their departure. It was unfortunate in the situation just described that the team member was not more responsive to the group's encouragement, but at the same time, group accountability avoided a subjective one-on-one encounter with the team leader (me) that might have resulted in political unrest in the church if some people had begun saying, "the pastor is not supportive of my favorite staff member."

Prayerful and sensitive leadership teams will make every effort to help a team member get on board with the rest of the team. If it seems apparent this is not possible, or the staff member is resistant, the team enters into prayer for that person and honestly dialogues about the person's role in the church. In the best cases, I have observed team members who did not fit in with a particular church leadership team to part in love and with dignity. I remember a woman who actually thanked the team for helping her clarify in her mind the kind of place she needed in a church to shine. That particular team prayed for her relocation and celebrated with her the discovery of a position that better fit her emerging spiritual identity and orientation to ministry.

Here are more advantages to creating group accountability:

- Team members become clear about their responsibilities and the ways their individual contribution fits into the team's total movement toward the vision of the church.

- Team members' performance is reviewed by the group not subjected to the opinions of a single person. Each team member has an ongoing dialogue about his or her work with the team that is dependant upon that work. Every team member implicitly inquires of the whole team: How can my gifts and passion for ministry best serve the interests of the leadership team in pursuing the church's vision?

- Team accountability tends to form clear team expectations and thus helps team members find their work meaningful and fulfilling. Potential new team members are interviewed by the team and either find the prospect of working in such a clearly defined, specific team environment thrilling or not, making it more likely that those who do join the team will work well within it.

Along with these advantages of team accountability, are two problems. However, they are resolvable. The first is that a church may benefit from an employee or volunteer who works best alone. Some people do not fit the team model yet are sincere disciples of Christ. Churches may want to design certain ministry positions to accommodate these personalities that require little accountability. I suggest, however, that a principal leader of the church should not be one of these personalities. A principal leader should be an essential part of the principal leadership team.

Second, leadership teams that are designed along the lines I am putting forth and that build strong accountability can become tyrannical. I cannot emphasize enough, then, the importance of prayer, Bible study, and the sincere application of Christian ethics in team life. Cohesive, collaborative, and effective ministry teams may not necessarily be godly. Teams that create strong team cultures must also institute in themselves a sense of humility, an awareness of human sin, and the conviction that each team member is a child of God. Church collaborative teams must seek to be like the house of love characterized in the perichoretic fellowship of God, seeking to do what they are called to do out of love. Love does not preclude efficiency, but it also does not require it. God's loving fellowship should be a team's highest aspiration.

Identify Dysfunction and Learn from It

Collaborative teams, immersed in the love of God, are gracious and forgiving teams whose members forgive one another and learn from failure. Human sin and pride are strong. We make mistakes. Team members may slip into gossip about each other, consciously or unconsciously sabotage each other's ministries, withhold important information, or otherwise act in ways that are spiritually dysfunctional for the group. The dysfunction we act out in the team is very likely the same kind we learned in our families of origins. Good leadership teams allow for such dysfunction, acknowledge it when it happens, forgive, and identify better ways of relating. Christian community must be marked by grace and exhibit that grace to the congregation as a model behavior. Otherwise a congregation can become filled with angry, unrelenting Pharisees.

As leaders build a collaborative leadership team, they must instill honesty and not be afraid to identify behaviors that work against the group. The team must discuss ways of improving group life that respect team members and that help each member be the person God is calling her or him to be. They must keep in front of them God's model to us of the Lord's own perichoretic fellowship, which moves and collaborates in love and truth.

Take Enough Time

The formation of collaborative teams takes time. Team members have to meet often with each other to be on the same track. Virtual meetings and e-mail and voice mail contacts are fine and good, but nothing replaces the time spent together in face-to-face meetings. Arriving at the collaborative edge where the clarity of the vision pursued, the strategy to pursue it, the sharing of passion about the vision, and the application of a variety of gifts in pursuit of the vision all come together takes time. Furthermore, church teams must pray together. As I have been emphasizing throughout, all the organizational theories and practical steps combined are insignificant if not combined with active prayer and commitment to the lordship of Jesus Christ. Collaborative church teams are prayerful teams that pray for church members and team members' personal needs and concerns as well as for the direction of the church and of the team itself. Collaborative church teams are continually seeking God's direction and seeking to stay in touch with the movement of the Spirit. These things take time—personal sharing, kneeling in prayer, Bible study and meditation, worship.

Team meetings, then, must be frequent and last for hours. I typically meet with my leadership team for half a day each week. The time is spent in praying and personal sharing, worshiping and Bible reading, planning, programming, strategizing, and communicating about the total program of the church. Once a month we share a meal together. Every six months we take a full day and go on retreat. Periodically we schedule an in-service training event to increase our knowledge and skills or assess our gifts. If the need is sensed, we invite outside consultants to guide us in a team-building exercise. Teams must take the time necessary to know one another, build camaraderie, and understand each member's passion, gifts, and spiritual journey.

The fruits of the time invested are plentiful. Conflict is minimized because people begin to understand each other better. Suspicion is like a balloon that deflates when people spend time in prayer and fellowship with one another. Often a suspicious person loses the image of another person as untrustworthy after the two spend time in prayer together, over a meal, or with each other's families. Collaboration is increased when team members spend enough time together to develop a good image of one another's strengths and passions. Casual conversation also has a wonderful effect of generating new creativity around programs and ministry. Some of the best ideas for ministry have surfaced at the coffee pot in the team room. Finally, teams that spend time together tend to develop relationships of a quality that has resounding positive effects throughout the congregation.

7

THE TRUSTING TEAM

CHURCH LEADERSHIP teams must model trust. They must work to keep it. When it is lost, they must work to regain it. Churches, like people, thrive and blossom in environments of trust and become ugly and schismatic when overwhelmed by distrust. Few things are more painful in relationships than broken trust, and few things are more difficult to repair. As with the other characteristics of effective church-based teams, the ways a church leadership team builds and retains trust among its members and exhibits trust to the church at large will determine, in large part, how well trust becomes a part of the total fabric of the congregation. Conversely, few things will devastate both a leadership team and a congregation quicker than the waves of suspicion and fear that follow in the wake of broken trust.

In this chapter I discuss the skill and art of developing trusting relationships in church leadership. On the one hand all the progress teams can make by covenanting, finding their vision, creating a culture, and collaborating can be easily undercut by distrust and suspicion. On the other hand how wonderful it is to worship with the people of God in a trusting environment that stands out in our incredibly suspicious world like a beacon of light in a raging storm. When it comes to trust, the stakes are huge.

The first definition of *trust* in *Merriam-Webster's Collegiate Dictionary* (10th ed.) is "assured reliance on the character, ability, strength, or truth of someone or something." Relationships cannot grow when there is no trust. We need to feel safe and secure with people and our environment. Without a strong sense of trust, we build walls, dig in, protect ourselves, live in suspicion, and are constantly in fear of an unpredictable world.

Abraham Maslow, Erik Erikson, and more recently James Fowler have written about the importance of trust development in infancy. Fowler (1981, pp. 120–121), in particular, related it to faith development. A young child who finds his or her environment to be trustworthy, dependable, and nurturing will tend to be able to trust in a God who gives assurances of ultimate safety in an uncertain world. Similarly, those raised in trustworthy environments tend to be better at building relationships of trust than those whose beginnings were couched in unpredictability.

Regardless of people's beginnings, however, I am convinced that a church that builds and maintains a strong culture of honesty and trust is able to encourage new attitudes of trust in otherwise suspicious and fearful people. Church leadership teams have a wonderful opportunity to model and inculcate trust and, in so doing, show the congregation honest and authentic ways of living the Christian life. Tremendous healing in the lives of people who have been shattered by broken trust is possible in such churches. And, like so many other important traits, trust begins with the leadership team.

While writing these chapters, I discussed their content with Constance Jordan-Haas, a Harvard Divinity School graduate and exceptional pastor on staff with me at Noroton Presbyterian Church in Darien, Connecticut, and she asked why this chapter on trust comes after the chapters on covenanting, vision seeking, culture creating, and collaborating when it is "so bedrock to developing strong faith and relationships." Other church leaders may have the same question, so let me explain.

The first four chapters of Part Two are skill oriented and specific. Here is a way to write a covenant, a process to perform a vision quest, a method of culture creating, and the things to do to collaborate. This chapter strikes me as different. Trust building is more elusive, more artful, and strikes to the heart of persons' psyches. Discussion of trust introduces a more serious note into what has so far been a rather delightful symphony of possibilities for leadership teams, and I hope that it has created a sense of enthusiasm about the good things leadership teams can do to help faithful congregations get focused and moving again. This chapter, however, is a shift in mood. Joy and many possibilities are still implied. But there is also a dangerous note. Here we come face to face with that which resulted in the Fall of humanity and separated us from our loving Creator who once walked in the Garden with us in perfect fellowship.

When we discuss trust we deal with the greatest possibilities—and the greatest threat—for leadership teams and congregations.

Unholy Suspicion

We return to First Church of Appleton as it is experiencing significant renewal. The leadership team covenant has formed the basis for improved relationships between once competing and conflicting staff members. The vision has united their energies and enthusiasm: they know what they are supposed to be doing and why. The culture creating is actually fun for them as they design worship services and programs and decorate church spaces to reflect their pursuit of God's cause. A new sense of meaning and fulfillment has come into the daily lives of church leaders, who see how their particular gifts and passions fit into ministry. Their collaboration has built camaraderie and community.

And then the serpent spoke.

To the pastoral care pastor: "You work and work, but look: the senior pastor gets the glory. He is rewarded more than anyone else for *your* hard labor."

To the youth pastor: "There's all this talk of team ministry and covenanting to be honest and open, but just look at that director of music. You know he's been accusing the youth program of snuffing out the youth choir. He's telling people you've gone too far in your programming, hogging the time youths are available and not leaving him any time for choir."

To the children's ministry pastor: "Your phones are probably bugged. I bet they're looking at your e-mail. They know you've been complaining to your colleagues in town that you're the lowest paid person on the leadership team. Better be careful what you say. Look! Someone is taking notes. Be careful!"

To the director of music: "They tell you you're safe, but you're not really. Church musicians come and go. Some of the team do not always like the music you prepare for worship. It's not the right mood or too traditional. You would be the first to go if the giving dropped. Why do you work so hard for such ungrateful people?"

To the senior pastor: "Some of the team members are not with you. Notice the way they ignore you in team meetings. When you talk about being a collaborative team, their eyes roll and burn. They're not with you. Better be careful of them. Find out what they're saying about you to other people."

Such are the seeds of distrust sown by the enemy. If the First Church leadership team or even a single team member allows them to take root, severe damage can result. The Tempter's words might lure some of the leaders to distrust one another, and over time some incidents might emerge that could be interpreted as betrayal, insensitivity, or personal competition. The leadership team could then drift further into separate camps and burning resentment.

However, if these feelings and incidents are brought up and openly discussed and the team works at overcoming them, the resulting trust earned will be highly rewarding. An added benefit will come as other church leaders who are aware of the potential problems observe the team members working through them in order to achieve a higher level of trust and community.

At this point, then, the First Church team is faced with a difficult but potentially wonderful opportunity: to share honestly and openly things that are almost too embarrassing to speak. When the difficult issues of relationships are broached and sensitively worked out, the resulting intimacy in community is tremendous. If First Church leaders were to "stuff" their anger, it could easily produce passive-aggressive behavior or simply result in reduced morale and enthusiasm for the mission cause.

As the First Church leaders encounter relational problems and questions of trust and endeavor honestly and openly to work through them as a team, a story of trust is established. Over time, the significant events when their relationships were tested and successfully worked become part of a history, a narrative of trust that is quite palpable. This trust legacy acts as a set of strong support pillars for the team culture and makes the team community inviting, warm, and safe.

I have known church workers who describe their workplaces as dark and foreboding. Walking into the church office is like descending into a tomb. The office is the repository of bad feelings produced by events that have disillusioned people and broken their trust. However, churches that have leaders who have managed to earn trust with each other are described as bright and welcoming. The office is an inviting place of fellowship and meaningful service to the Lord.

I have experienced the darkening sensation myself. Conflict produced anxiety in me that colored how I viewed my work and office. Opening the front door to the office felt terrifying. Yet I was determined not to let it master me. Naming the "demons," shedding light on the darkness, getting difficult issues out in the open, can be like an exorcism of those things that could tear up a fellowship of leaders. As teams deal with hard issues, the darkness lifts, and the environment becomes safe and inviting again. If the darkness is not lifted, however, it tends to spread to the whole church.

The Serpent in the Garden

Trust is a principal theme in Scripture. In fact, the sin that resulted in the Fall is that of distrusting God and asserting ourselves as gods instead. We betrayed the Creator of all—twice. First in the Garden of Eden and again in the Garden of Gethsemane.

Our Lord created all that is and set it before us in wonder and beauty and gave it all to us, simply requiring one thing. "And the Lord God commanded the man, 'You may freely eat of every tree of the garden; but of the tree of the knowledge of good and evil you shall not eat, for in the day that you eat of it you shall die'" (Gen. 2:16–17).

The serpent tempted Eve. He tried to quote God. Just as the tempter in the wilderness quoted Scripture to Jesus, so the serpent appeared pious, wondering what it was God really said. "Now the serpent was more crafty than any other wild animal that the Lord God had made. He said to the woman, 'Did God say, "You shall not eat from any tree in the garden?"'" (3:1).

The serpent quoted God out of context, twisting God's nature to appear less benevolent and more demanding. Eve corrected it, saying to the serpent, "We may eat of the fruit of the trees in the garden; but God said, 'You shall not eat of the fruit of the tree that is in the middle of the garden, nor shall you touch it, or you shall die'" (3:2–3).

God had expressed the gift of creation in an extremely positive way, emphasizing the gift of the trees of the garden, only of this one tree, the Lord forbade them to eat. The reason for the Lord's prohibition was love and concern for the human creatures who would find the fruit poisonous, as indeed we discovered.

The serpent continued to challenge God's good nature. It darkened Eve's mind and stirred up thoughts of distrust. "But the serpent said to the woman, 'You will not die; for God knows that when you eat of it your eyes will be opened, and you will be like God, knowing good and evil'" (3:4–5).

The serpent tempted Eve to distrust God. The Lord is not really for you. God is not on your side. You have been lied to. God is threatened by you and so has forbidden you to eat of the very tree that would make you like God. God has coerced you into not eating of this fine tree by threatening you with death, when in fact, it is life giving. So said the serpent of ancient times.

The great distrust of God in the Garden of Eden resulted not only in enmity between us and God but also between us and one another. The work of Jesus Christ to withstand the pious, Scripture-quoting devil and defeat the serpent's power on the cross means that we have peace with God and, potentially, peace with one another. The re-creation of trust between us and God—initiated and made possible by God—results in not only hope for renewed individuals but hope for renewed community. The Spirit of God in our midst works to unite us to one another and to God and reestablish the bonds of love and trust.

A People Called to Live in Trust

Since the Fall, God has been at work to restore the fellowship broken in the garden. The invitation to the fellowship, intimacy, movement, dance, joy, and community of God is reextended to us in Jesus Christ, Savior of the world. The cross restores the pathway to God. Members of churches are a people called to live forth this new community—new creation—in the world. The Spirit binds us to one another, makes our fellowship possible, and sends us as witnesses to the life-saving, community-creating Lord of lords.

Paul Hanson (1986) has traced the development of community in the Old and New Testaments and offers us wonderful word pictures of what biblical community looks like. He notes how covenants were developed (a form of trust making), how they were broken by Israel (broken trust), and how they were then reestablished in various ways through the prophets. Climactically, in both the teaching and life witness of Jesus Christ, the divine community is exhibited, and there is hope for its restoration. Hanson observes:

> Indivisibly related to Jesus' teaching the way of the Kingdom was his manifesting the way of the Kingdom in his own life. In his miracles, in his forgiveness of sins, in his style of reaching out to and drawing into his fellowship all manner of people, his disciples recognized the advent of God's reign. . . .
>
> This recognition led the followers of Jesus to confess that in Jesus God was present, drawing a lost human family back to fellowship with God, and healing a broken creation [p. 413].

The followers of Jesus believed then and now that the Spirit of God was upon him to live and proclaim the Kingdom of God—the new community, the new order, of God. We place our trust in Christ as one who reestablishes the covenant between us and God and restores the trust. And though we find ourselves unable to live the beauty of this new community by ourselves, we have been given the Spirit of God to restore and remind us of the perichoretic fellowship of God. The Spirit moves between the persons of God and between God and the people called to forge community and trust. What we are unable to do so by ourselves, God can work through us by the power and presence of the Spirit. We are not left "orphaned" (John 14:18) but are bound by the Spirit into a family of faith lifted into the fellowship of God because of the Savior, Jesus Christ. Hanson tells us:

Disciples in an often inhospitable environment need the support of others who share their vision, and who derive sustenance from their relationship to God, as experienced especially in common worship and prayer. This grounding in God and in God's righteous order give the faithful strength to stand united in their testimony that what multitudes call real is ultimately illusory, and that what to many seems illusory is the "pearl of great price."

In many ways, and in all types of life experiences, the individual believer is thus sustained within a community whose *trustworthiness* is not the product of human virtue, but of the mutual respect and caring that arises out of the common acknowledgement of God's sole sovereignty [p. 502; emphasis added].

The church is the place where this new community is called to come about, and the people who seek to lead such churches must work to experience the presence of the trust-making Spirit of God. In the leadership teams' living narratives of trust established, broken by human sin and weakness, but restored again by grace, congregations witness the transforming power of the Spirit and derive a sense of hope for their own lives, families, communities, and church at large.

The Trustworthy Perichoresis of God

The driving theological theme of this book—that in the church is the image of the Trinity, God as Father, Son, and Spirit in perichoretic fellowship—is not new. It is implied throughout Scripture where the Trinity of God emerges. It was also a part of the thinking and reasoning of early Christian leaders. I have already mentioned John of Damascus, but others have alluded to this theological theme of the church as the Trinitarian image of God.

Miroslav Volf's new book, *After Our Likeness: The Church as the Image of the Trinity* (1998), seems to lend some theological support to what I have aspired to demonstrate in this book. Volf, professor of systematic theology at Fuller Theological Seminary in Pasadena, California, seeks to give a Trinitarian theological grounding to Protestant *free church* thinking about the church. (It is also of interest to me that the cover of Volf's book shows the Rublev Trinity icon that I too have found meaningful and that his book is the first in a series with the title *Sacra Doctrina: Christian Theology for a Postmodern Age*.) The notion of taking a close look at Trinitarian theology to support the communal life of the church in postmodern society, although not new, seems to be gaining popularity on a wider scale and reaching beyond those denominations (for example, Roman Catholic and Eastern Orthodox) most likely to support it. My contribution as a pastor has been to look at ways to live out this theology *practically* in churches seeking to relate to the postmodern world.

Volf recognizes that on one hand the perichoretic fellowship of God is not possible in human communities because it is so utterly divine. As J. Moltmann observes, "By the power of their eternal love, the divine persons exist so intimately with, for, and in one another that they themselves constitute themselves in their unique, incomparable and complete union" (quoted in Volf, p. 210). On the other hand God makes possible a kind of mutual giving and receiving, imaged in the fellowship of the Father, Son, and Spirit. "In personal encounters, that which the other person is flows consciously or unconsciously into that which I am. The reverse is also true. In this mutual giving and receiving, we give to others not only something, but also a piece of ourselves, something of that which we have made of ourselves in communion with others; and from others we take not only something, but also a piece of them" (Volf, p. 211).

This concept of the perichoretic fellowship of God enabled in the church runs contrary to the rugged individualism valued in Western society. God creates the persons of the church to be in fellowship with one another in a way that creates communities of trust, covenant, and love. These communities are made up of people interdependent on one another. They are not independent of one another, which ruins community. And they are not dependent on one another to the degree that they take on a cultlike conformity that blurs each person's God-given peculiarities. Rather, God forms people into interdependent communities of give and take, mutual giving and receiving, that are the basis for relationships of trust and covenant. Although a human community of trust is not exactly like the organic unity of the one God in three persons, it is, nonetheless, in the image of God insofar as its members love, share, and trust.

The practical living out of this community (described in more detail later in this chapter) focuses on the honesty made possible by the Spirit in the church. We have no sense at all of God hiding God's self from God. God is perfectly and wonderfully who God is within the community of God's own being. This mutuality, sharing, giving, intimacy, and love of God exhibits to us possibilities for our community of authentic honesty. This honesty does not rest on feigned perfection ("trust me because I am trustworthy in every way") but rather openness of need ("trust me because I am seeking to be honest about myself and my need for grace"). What hope we have for living perichoretic fellowship in leadership teams and modeling it to the church at large is the hope we have for authentic and genuine honesty. The degree to which honesty is broached in human community is the degree to which we tend to experience the ability of the Spirit of God to forgive and transcend our brokenness, in process of repair, and weave us into intimate fellowship.

Workplace Teams Built on Trust

People today hunger for authentic relationships. They have been conned enough. The words *trust, honesty, truth,* and *integrity* are thrown around with apparent ease, but the living out of them is shallow or nonexistent. We live in the wake of high-profile politicians, ministers, and evangelists who have lied and deceived.

In the corporate and organizational realm, postmodern people are searching for more meaningful work communities, ones in which trust can be established and in which mutual giving and receiving in relationships exists.

Margaret Wheatley (1992) has recognized this growing need, noting people's shift from looking for external rewards to looking for internal rewards. She tells us: "In motivational theory, our attention is shifting from the enticement of external rewards to the intrinsic motivators that spring from the work itself. We are refocusing on the deep longings we have for community, meaning, dignity, and love in our organizational lives" (p. 12). People need to be valued, involved, respected, and afforded a sense of dignity as they collaborate to accomplish something meaningful. The old styles of corporate bullying are not effective. "For many years, the prevailing maxim of management stated: 'Management is getting work done through others.' The important thing was the work; the 'others' were nuisances that needed to be managed into conformity and predictability. Managers have recently been urged to notice that they have *people* working for them. They have been advised that work gets done by humans like themselves, each with strong desires for recognition and connectedness. The more they [we] feel part of the organization, the more work gets done" (p. 144).

People have a greater need today for environments that build trust, integrity, and honesty. Many in the business world are learning that such environments increase movement toward both material and spiritual goals. Not only is work better and more efficient, but a quality of community is developed that increases individuals' satisfaction with the human and spiritual values in their work.

Southwest Airlines has experienced phenomenal success in business partly because of the trusting environment created for employees. It is trust "fed by personal integrity. Trust grows when we keep our promises and follow through our commitments. You have to be deadly earnest, completely authentic, and do what you say you are going to do to earn people's trust" (Freiberg and Freiberg, 1996, p. 109). This kind of attitude and managerial practice has helped Southwest's management negotiate long-term union contracts with pilots that represented "a significant departure from industry norms. Southwest pilots would have been unwilling to take the risks associated with such a long-term commitment had there not been years of trust built up between them and management" (p. 108). Trust at Southwest is not a hope, slogan, or promise. It is the way day-to-day life is lived out. Commenting, in effect, on the narrative formed by a tradition of events that have demonstrated trust and integrity, Jim Wimberly, Southwestern vice president of ground operations has remarked, "It's the way you treat people on a daily basis that impacts the degree of success you have when you officially sit down to work out a contract" (p. 108).

Although trust building is finding new value in U.S. organizations and business, the absence of trust continues to be a significant problem in every community. As I described earlier, this is a deep and abiding human problem. Kouzes and Posner (1995), for example, cite a number of studies that show the impact of the loss of trust and offer one particularly frightening description of organizational life when trust is lost between organizational leaders. The chilling description exactly fits experiences I have had and that have been shared with me by other pastors and Christian leaders.

In one study (Boss, 1978), groups of business executives were formed as part of a role-playing exercise in trust and management leadership. The task of the groups was to solve a complex manufacturing problem. Some of the groups were briefed to expect trusting behavior ("You have learned from your past experiences that you can trust the other members of top management and can openly express feelings and differences with them"). The others were told to expect untrusting behavior.

The groups engaged in their task for only thirty minutes when asked to complete a brief questionnaire. Both team members and observers of the individual teams completed the same questionnaire. The groups that were told their "managers" could be trusted rated their experience positively on every factor evaluated. The groups that were told that their leaders could not be trusted had an entirely different experience. Distrust grew so strong that group members distorted the sincere attempts of their "managers" and thought they were being deceived. Managers of these groups grew frustrated and angry as their group members worked to sabotage their efforts to lead the groups in problem solving.

Kouzes and Posner (1995), reflecting on this study, find it remarkable that the difficulties associated with distrust can emerge so evidently in a thirty-minute simulation. They observe that trust is the "most significant predictor of individuals' satisfaction with their organization" (p. 165). Simply the suggestion of distrust can infect a work group, resulting in twisted facts and distorted perceptions. Distrust creates a climate of suspicion resulting in misunderstanding and fear. People become highly territorial and protective, which results in lower productivity and severely weakened morale. My experience parallels that of other pastors who have labored sincerely to draw another person into a creative, collaborative work relationship. Yet because rumor or innuendo creates an atmosphere of distrust, that person stared with steely eyes and refused to participate. How difficult it is to work through these situations!

The first priority of any leader is to establish trust. And in those terrible times when trust gets stretched or broken, the leader must work to reestablish trust. Trust is an essential currency in community relationships without which no changes can be purchased.

Jon Katzenbach and Douglas Smith (1994) also find that high-performance teams require high-level trust: "Of the risks required [to form work teams], the most formidable involve building the trust and interdependence necessary to move from individual accountability to mutual accountability. People on real teams must trust and depend on one another—not totally or forever—but certainly with respect to the team's purpose, performance goals, and approach. For most of us such trust and interdependence do not come easily" (p. 109).

Building and maintaining trust are not easy, but trust is essential to organizational life today. In the next section, I suggest ways for leaders and leadership teams to form the trust teams require to be effective in the postmodern world.

Building Trusting Teams

The following suggestions are a combination of, first, spiritual disciplines and, second, action steps that leadership teams can undertake to build and maintain trusting relationships.

Pray

When Isaiah beheld the glory of God in the Temple he confessed, "Woe is me! I am lost, for I am a man of unclean lips, and I live among a people of unclean lips; yet my eyes have seen the King, the Lord of hosts!" (Isa. 6:5). When Peter realized that Jesus was no ordinary rabbi, he fell down at Jesus' knees, saying, "Go away from me, Lord, for I am a sinful man!" (Luke 5:8). It is difficult to remain proud in the presence of God! In prayer, we fellowship with God and become deeply aware of our need for grace. The humility attendant on an active life of prayer enables team members better to approach one another, aware of their mutual brokenness. This check on human pride is a prerequisite for the kind of honesty that builds trust.

Read Scripture Daily

We must immerse ourselves in biblical culture in order to begin to live it. The Kingdom culture Jesus teaches and embodies must become the culture we emulate. Leslie Newbigin (1989) stresses how important it is that communities of faith actually *indwell* the Bible in order "to seek to understand and cope with what is out there [in a pluralist society]." From Scripture, "we get a picture of the Christian life as one in which we live *in* the biblical story as part of the community whose story it is, find in the story the clues to knowing God as his character becomes manifest in the story, and from within that indwelling try to understand and cope with the events of our time and the world about us and so carry the story forward" (p. 99; emphasis added).

Immersing ourselves in Scripture is a way to be continually reminded by the Spirit of the things of God and the Kingdom we are called to live forth in our ministries.

Be Honest and Truthful

Leadership teams simply must not tolerate lying, deceiving, and gossip. When such things arise, they must be named and talked about. We are guilty of all of them to a degree and must keep each other accountable to a higher way of living.

Honesty extends beyond simply telling the truth. It also means taking risks to be honest about one's resentments and anger that could otherwise infect the team with something poisonous. Perceptions of betrayal or injustice lodge themselves in our hearts and keep us from full team participation and trust until they are dislodged. To begin to show them to the team requires remarkable courage; courage that should be rewarded by the rest of the team and lifted up as an example for all to follow.

Neely Towe has been pastor for nine years of the highly innovative Stanwich Congregational Church in Greenwich, Connecticut. She puts a high premium on trust. "The confidence that we find in God's grace allows us to be vulnerable. If we are not safe with God, then we have to self-protect, we have to be right. When being right is more important than loving, then you've lost it." She told me her formula for helping her team build such trust and vulnerability: "We do a lot of praying together. We do a lot of repenting. We hold each other accountable."

Towe also comments that "the first principle of leadership is being trustworthy. If trust is broken, it is the hardest thing to restore." This trust is established and preserved over time by being honest. It also means being confidential with information shared with teams in confidence. "One of the most serious ways trust is broken is not keeping things confidential," she says.

I happened to be preaching one Sunday in the church where Towe is pastor. During the time of prayer I overheard the faint voice of associate pastor Joan Osgood praying softly and sincerely, interceding for her pastor, Neely. Her prayer was for me a symbol of the kind of love and community pastors and leadership teams can model to their congregations.

Reward the Truth-Teller

Teams must make heroes and heroines out of those who risk telling the truth. It must be clear, even stated in the team's written covenant, that no team member will be penalized for telling the truth. Pastors and team leaders must not use the honesty of team members to discredit them. Team members must keep such honesty confidential and not embarrass the truth-teller. If any news of such bravery is going to be shared with people outside the team, it should take the form of a message, which all team members have agreed on, saying how grateful the leadership team is to the person who was willing to risk honesty so that the team might better function in the ministry cause. If anything, truth-tellers should be considered valiant.

The truth-teller may not be correct in his perception, but the beginning of correcting that perception is expressing it to others. The team as a whole can affirm or correct the perception as it is revealed. As discussed in relation to collaborative teams, a person's honesty about problems with the team may never result in peace or harmony within the team for that person. However, the person, in loving dialogue with the other team members, may come to a beneficial realization that another place would be better suited to his gifts.

Denny Bellesi, pastor of Coast Hills Community Church in Aliso Viejo, California, has told me about a similar experience he had with a member of his leadership team. The church was going through a series of needed changes, with the result that some team members wondered if they still fit the culture of the church. Bellesi felt a deep loyalty to his team, and he worked hard with team members to help them fit into the changing culture, but one person was not able to make the change. He told Bellesi, "This is not the best place for me. I have a vision of my own of who I am and where God wants me." He eventually found a better environment for his passion and gifts.

Learn from Failures

Learning to live in community by building trust relationships is a difficult enterprise that takes time. Teams and team members should not let past failures overwhelm them with guilt. They should learn from them and let the Spirit work to improve their ability to both trust and be trustworthy.

Suzanne House Ebel has served as a pastor on several leadership teams over her career as a Presbyterian minister. She has learned a lot about what makes for harmonious teams from the instances of failure she has witnessed in trust building. "I've had two experiences on church staffs as an associate pastor that were quite difficult," she recalled to me. One situation offered a harmony of vision, goals, and strategy for ministry. What was lacking was honest sharing. "Staff members wanted to accomplish the same things, yet there were constant misunderstandings going on. The problem was an unwillingness to talk it out. In my personal experience, if leaders are not honest and vulnerable with one another, ministry suffers." In another case, lack of quality communication and honest sharing escalated into a problem throughout the church: "A distrust among the church's staff and elders led to factions, triangulation, and undermining of one another's ministries. Church leaders were discrediting one another to the church at large. It was a very painful experience that caused me to struggle with anger and grieve for the loss of the overall mission of the Church of Jesus Christ."

Years ago I was invited by Leadership Network to meet in Colorado Springs with some of America's most innovative pastors to discuss ministry. I would be in the company of people who had built huge churches from nothing and who were noted for some highly creative forms of outreach and mission, and on the flight to Colorado Springs, I wondered what most of these leaders would be like. Would they brag about their accomplishments? Would our peer learning sessions be marked by "my church is bigger than your church" competitive talk? I wasn't sure what to expect. What I discovered, however, were honest and sincere church leaders who had as much to share about their faults and failures as their successes. In fact, I found some of them reluctant to say anything remotely similar to a boast. Unless you knew it from another source, you might not even know that they led some of the largest, most vibrant fellowships in the country. I learned as much from hearing about their failures as about their innovative successes. I also felt free to share my own sense of inadequacy and my failures because they were willing to share theirs.

Meet Often

Leadership teams that build trust are teams that spend time together. There is no substitute for this time together. Trust is dependant upon a narrative of events that builds up the team's identity and confidence. Those events will be both serious and playful. The serious events will be the ones in which the team worked through crisis and brutally honest sharing. The playful events will be the ones in which the team learned about one another's gifts, personalities, and approaches to life.

Walt Kallestad works hard to maintain a community of trust at what has become a huge church, Community of Joy in Glendale, Arizona. Speaking of his staff, Kallestad told me, "We value relationships. We go to lunch regularly. We have gone together for a staff retreat to Disneyland and to Universal Studios. We play together, go to the movies, and have parties together to build a highly relational staff." And he wonders how any team could do differently and still build trust. "How in the world could a football or basketball team not meet often? It would be chaos out there on the field!"

Don't Underestimate Trust Building

Becoming trustworthy is different from vision casting or culture creating. The latter are things we *do*. Being trustworthy is something we *are*. And that trustworthiness is then demonstrated in what we say and do over time. We must keep focused on being trustworthy as individual team members and as a team. We have to work at speaking clearly about who we are and what is important to us. We have to keep our promises and do what we say we will do. We must show respect to other team members; be honest and vulnerable; and not hide behind credentials, titles, accomplishments, and vestments. Our goal is not to be perfect, but authentic. Think and pray about these things daily and be intentional about them. When they are nonexistent in our teams, then our teamwork will never flourish. It will never dramatically influence the wider church and community that hungers for perichoretic truthfulness.

8

THE EMPOWERING TEAM

EFFECTIVE MINISTRY teams in the church in the postmodern era are empowering teams. They have put aside the older, hierarchical models and spread out the authority and responsibility of doing ministry. Leadership no longer means taking control, dictating, or giving orders. Gone also are the more subtle forms of controlling, such as using theological degrees to lift oneself above others with the implication that "clergy know best." Those who engage in theological and biblical study, and earn the related credentials, will continue to be very important servants of the church for helping people *reflect* on the nature of God and the practice of ministry. But they ought not to take the responsibility for *doing* ministry or *thinking* about ministry away from the people. On the contrary, because of the strong biblical support for the ministry of the people, those theologically trained find it their responsibility to emphasize the growth and development of the people of the church into ministers of the Gospel.

In fact, I believe that mainline churches and denominations are wonderfully poised for the twenty-first century—*if they would make important changes of the kind suggested here.* Their emphasis on theological reflection and biblical exegesis could help ground the popular Bible-based, independent churches and the *new paradigm churches* (Miller, 1997), such as Vineyard Fellowship, Hope Chapel, and Calvary Chapel, in a traditional and historical framework. This grounding need not stifle innovative Christian movements or pastors (those whom Michael Slaughter, 1994, calls *spiritual entrepreneurs*). Innovation in ministry can occur even as those engaging in it constantly reflect on it theologically and biblically. Good theological reflection and historical analysis can ground faith that otherwise might become superficial, faith in danger of becoming religious entertainment, and at worst, spiritual excesses that manipulate congregations and lead them into cultism. On the other side, as the mainline theological traditions offer the helpful gift of theological reflection, care must be taken that excessive analysis does not paralyze innovators in ministry, because not acting and not taking risks always appear theologically safer than venturing out into the swirling postmodern world of change. What is needed is a careful balance between innovation and tradition.

One of the marks of highly innovative and life-filled churches today is the giving away of ministry to the people in ways that resemble the ministry of the early church. Clerics in these churches function as coaches, giving advice to, equipping, training, and encouraging those in the front lines of ministry: the people. This is not a new idea. I have described how clergy-dominated styles of ministry arose out of the European parish model (sometimes referred to as the *chaplaincy model*). In this model, the pastor or priest acts as chaplain to the parish. He runs around to make sure his flock is spiritually fed and taken care of. He baptizes, marries, buries, and otherwise performs the essential functions of the church. In times of trouble, he visits the sick and the poor and offers needed counsel. After all, he is *trained* and he is *educated* and he has special *credentials* and he is *paid* to do these things.

In this way, the pastor or priest slowly took on more and more of the responsibility of the parish, becoming the sole "vendor" of spirituality. The laity, even the elders and deacons, were reduced to board members who tended to abdicate authority because it was easier to let the trained cleric do the ministry of the church. When the ordained laity did assert authority, it was usually to shape policy and settle disputes rather than to innovate new ministries.

The church in the postmodern world must return the ministry to the people. The church began as a populist movement led by a servant-messiah who crossed the religious authorities to bring genuine faith back to the people. If churches are to have meaning in the postmodern world it will be because they are filled with people who have experienced that populist meaning, claim it, and are willing to live it in the world. The clergy must get out of the way of the people and encourage them on!

The Apple Growers of Appleton

In Appleton the First Church leadership team has made significant changes to become more effective and spiritually meaningful. They have covenanted together and experienced some of the difficulties of actually living out that covenant. Their vision is firmly before them. They have created a team culture that reinforces that vision, and team members have worked to understand one another's gifts and passions in order to increase team collaboration. Having lived through some crises and shared hard knowledge about their relationships, they have begun to establish a narrative of trust that has deepened their community life.

The First Church leaders now have a wonderful opportunity to seed their community. There is no specific time or chronology for a team such as this one to begin creating other ministry teams (a principal way of enabling lay ministry). This process can begin as soon as its value is recognized. However, in churches used to other models of ministry, it is helpful for the principal leadership group to become covenanting, vision seeking, culture creating, and collaborative first. When the other church leaders and members witness the change in the leadership team, they will be more inclined to support the development of other ministry teams in the church, using the leadership team as a model. Thus, much depends upon the principal leaders' success as a team. Conversely, much can be unraveled if they fail as a team.

All along, the First Church leadership team will have been teaching the laity about their ministry through Bible studies, topical classes, and all the communication media of the church. One of the emphases of the First Church vision was to equip and enable the congregation for ministry. Now this vision statement begins to become a reality.

One of the most important places for First Church to seed team ministry is the church board. Most traditional churches have boards (or sessions, or vestries) organized around a committee structure. Each board committee recommends policy for its area of ministry to the full board. The board is led by a chairperson who oversees orderly committee operation. The agenda for a typical board meeting calls for reviewing the minutes of the previous meeting, acting on committee recommendations, discussing any new business the board might want to consider, and then adjourning. A "good" chairperson is one who does not allow the meeting to last too long. First Church would change this pattern.

After months of teaching the importance of a biblical, team-based approach to ministry, and having modeled that approach and given witness to its success, the First Church of Appleton leadership team works with the board to reform it into a team. The board chooses to adopt the leadership team covenant as a guide for its own relationships, making some adjustments for its unique fellowship. Board members have already walked with the leadership team through a vision-seeking process, been influenced by the team's culture creating, and admired team efforts to collaborate and build trust. These qualities have inspired the board to be like the leadership team.

At a weekend retreat, the leadership team worked with the board to help it change to a team-based model. Its name was changed from the First Church of Appleton Board of Elders to the Apple Core Team. Board committee names were changed to team names. For example, the Worship Committee became the Praise and Prayer Celebration Team and the Christian Education Committee became the Disciple Making Team. Committee chairs became team leaders.

During the retreat, the board teams met in separate rooms to devise team goals that would fit within the larger vision of the church. They also specified measurable action steps for reaching those goals. These action steps could later form the basis for evaluation of each team's work.

Reconvening as a whole, the Apple Core Team reviewed the goals and action steps of each ministry team and adopted them, with various amendments, into a cohesive strategy for the ministry of the congregation.

Key to the First Church strategy of ministry was the acknowledgment of the ministry of the laity. The position of volunteer coordinator was established for the purpose of developing a database of gifts and passions among church members and plugging them into ministries. Each ministry team had a central person (or coordinating team) that team members could go to with recruitment needs. The congregation was strongly urged by the leadership team and the Apple Core Team to be involved in at least one ministry enterprise of the church. The volunteer coordinator was available to help people determine their gifts and passions and to match them with the appropriate ministry teams.

The Apple Core Team also began acting with less suspicion toward those who wanted to start new ministries. Rather than run individuals' proposals through a maze of committee and board approvals, the Apple Core Team set up a point person who could quickly determine if proposed new ministry endeavors (and subsequent teams for those ministries) fit the vision and culture of the church. People could get permission to act as a church-based ministry team more quickly, though the Apple Core Team set up criteria to ensure that such teams did not venture too far out on their own.

Training became a high priority. An active laity needs to be resourced and supported in its ministries. The Apple Core Team established training seminars that equipped people for specific ministry areas. The *seed casters* were ministry innovators who were trained in establishing ministry teams to meet new needs. The *planters* were trained for the ministry of disciple making: leading new members of the church through a series of classes and experiences to deepen their roots in their Christian faith and understanding. The *fertilizers* were entrusted with the ministry of growing up a generation of new leaders for ministry teams. The *harvesters* were those gifted in evangelism. *Graduates* of training in these ministry areas were available to lead a variety of ministry teams that could pursue specific ministry causes.

Over time, First Church discovered the value of cell teams. These small communities of about ten people each were designed as Bible study and prayer groups that provided community, accountability, emotional support, spiritual growth, and mission outreach. Each of these small communities could function like a ministry team (for example, a pastoral care team). It could take on a ministry cause that was under the overall vision and umbrella of the church. All the features of a ministry team could be found in the small community, but each community had the added feature of developing the faith and spiritual disciplines of its members. At First Church these small communities were called *orchards*. At first, they were identified by types of apples: the Red Delicious Orchard, the McIntosh Orchard, and so forth. When they ran out of types of apples, they began to name themselves after biblical people: David's Orchard and Rebecca's Grove and the like.

The Apple Core Team meetings hardly resembled the former First Church board meetings. After the opening prayer and devotional time, the pastor shared with the board the continuing importance of being team based and of constantly working to reinforce that concept. After his comments, an omnibus motion quickly dispensed with routine business. The recommendations involved had been sent in advance to board members along with supporting materials. They could easily be passed without discussion, although a board member could pull one for debate if he or she thought necessary. Finishing quickly the actions necessary for the maintenance of the organization, the board was propelled into a lively review of its progress toward various ministry goals, including its overall vision. For example, the Praise and Celebration Team (formerly the Worship Committee) reported on its work in developing worship services that communicated vital faith. The Christian Nurture Team shared its joy about its work on developing a comprehensive plan to deepen the faith and community life of the membership. The Mission Team told of the many new ministries involved in living out faith in the community.

The otherwise boring parliamentary proceedings were transformed into strategy discussions for moving ahead with pertinent plans of ministry and mission. The setting was transformed from a staid, boring boardroom where elders watched their watches to a vibrant, energized team environment.

Another big change at First Church took place in the Apple Seed Class (formerly the New Members Class). In prior years staff had told the history of First Church of Appleton in this class, noting its proud heritage in the community and mentioning the various pastors that had served it and the dates when the buildings were completed (as if the church were defined by pastors and buildings). The various ministries were discussed, with emphasis on the programs that were especially good and tended to draw new people. A pledge card for financial contributions was distributed along with a membership form to be filled out. And a final word of encouragement was said: "And we hope you will enjoy your new church home."

The Apple Seed Class was entirely different. First, the newcomers were shown the essential vision of the church and told, "This is what we are about and where we are going." This was followed by a discussion of the culture of the church; a video summarizing the team model, with footage of a typical ministry community (or orchard) and a strong suggestion that new members join one (orchard materials and sign-up cards were passed out); slides about foreign and domestic missions and the difference the church was making in the lives of people; a quick virtual tour of the various team mission goals that naturally flowed from the central vision of the church; an admonition that to be a member of First Church of Appleton was to be expected to be involved in spiritual disciplines and team ministry; and the distribution of a CD-ROM that reviewed most of what the Apple Seed Class covered (the material was also on the church Web site). In forty-five minutes, those in the Apple Seed Class knew exactly what the church was about and how it was going about accomplishing its mission, and they had heard a call to be involved "because Christ calls us to be the church together in ministry and *you* have a unique and important part to play in that ministry."

Amid all the other changes, the church changed its name. First Church of Appleton, located at 22 Apple Hill Way, became the Apple Hill Church.

Postmodern Romans

Postmodern people need to feel involved. They need a sense that they are participating in the vital aspects of a cause. The church needs to accommodate this need, not because the church should accommodate culture but *because it is the right thing to do*. As I have argued repeatedly, changing to fit culture in these key areas actually contributes to the reformation of the church along good, strong biblical and theological lines. It takes us back to who we once were in the first century A.D. We get back to being a church that resembles fellowships described in the acts of the Apostles and their epistles. Indeed, the culture of the Roman Empire was similar to our postmodern culture. As the Romans linked together many new cultures around the Mediterranean, they melded into a kind of pluralist society, not unlike our postmodern culture. New religious and philosophical thinking flooded the empire's experience. There was a crisis of meaning as people searched for that which was ultimate. It is in such a climate that Christianity flourishes. It flourishes because it is true and is able to meet the spiritual hunger of people caught in orders that no longer have meaning. It flourishes because it brings a strong message of hope to communities that have lost hope. What a wonderful time it is for the church today; a time full of opportunities to spread the Gospel person to person.

The Body of Christ in the Postmodern Age

The book of Genesis, in its word picture of God's original design, gives us a clue about the kind of relationship we are called to have with one another and with creation.

After creating all that is, God said to the human creatures:

> "Be fruitful and multiply, and fill the earth and subdue it; and have
> dominion over the fish of the sea and over the birds of the air and over
> every living thing that moves upon the earth." God said, "See, I have
> given you every plant yielding seed that is upon the face of all the earth,
> and every tree with seed in its fruit; you shall have them for food. And
> to every beast of the earth, and to every bird of the air, and to every-
> thing that creeps on the earth, everything that has the breath of life, I
> have given every green plant for food." And it was so [Gen. 1:28–30].

Commenting on this passage, Walter Brueggemann (1982) suggests that a consensus exists about what it means to be made in the "image of God," as stated in Genesis. Brueggemann says it is like the situation of the king who set up statues of himself to assert his lordship where he himself was not present. "The human creature attests to the Godness of God by exercising *freedom with* and *authority over* all the other creatures entrusted to its care. The image of God in the human person is a mandate of power and responsibility."

This might sound, at first, rather hostile and even bring to mind images of tyranny, of Hitler and Stalin. But Brueggemann suggests otherwise. The responsibility (dominion) and power human beings have been given is "a power exercised as God exercises power." We are created in the image of God, in this regard, by having "the creative use of power which invites, evokes, and permits. There is nothing here of coercive or tyrannical power, either for God or for humankind" (p. 32).

Even in the phrase "dominion over," Brueggemann does not find justification for the wanton exploitation of people or nature. "The dominance is that of a shepherd who cares for, tends, and feeds the animals," he writes. "Thus the task of 'dominion' does not have to do with exploitation and abuse. It has to do with securing the well-being of every other creature and bringing the promise of each to full fruition" (p. 32).

Genesis gives us clues about the ways power and dominion are to be exercised in human community. But if we had any doubts, Jesus is our model of how we are to be with one another. Jesus comes to us as the suffering servant of God who laid down his life for his friends and who served and taught and loved us to wholeness. Jesus models for us the washing of the feet of disciples and shows us that lordship is costly and full of self-denial. Jesus, the Son of God, God incarnate, models for us the image of power we are to have with one another: stooped down and washing feet, shepherding, giving, being last, and serving. These are the power and dominion images in the Church of Jesus Christ.

As mentioned in the Chapter Six, William Easum (1995) believes that Paul's description of the church as the body of Christ is highly relevant for churches in the postmodern age (what he and Margaret Wheatley (1992) call the *quantum age*). He argues passionately for the church to reorganize itself around cell groups and *permission-giving* networks. These networks match Paul's description of the body of Christ.

> Indeed, the body does not consist of one member but of many. If the foot would say, "Because I am not a hand, I do not belong to the body," that would not make it any less a part of the body. And if the ear would say, "Because I am not an eye, I do not belong to the body," that would not make it any less a part of the body. If the whole body were an eye, where would the hearing be? If the whole body were hearing, where would the sense of smell be? But as it is, God arranged the members in the body, each one of them, as he chose. If all were a single member, where would the body be? As it is, there are many members, yet one body [1 Cor. 12:14–20].

The concept of the church as the body of Christ evokes, according to Easum, images that fit well in a quantum age. He notes that the human body has a hundred trillion cells and "each type of cell works independently of other cells but always on behalf of the well-being of the entire body" (p. 42). It is hard to develop tyrannical models of power based on the human body. "The body is a bottom-up network based on cooperation, freedom, and the common good" (p. 43). Similarly, "individual members of the Body of Christ find their fulfillment, not as their ministry makes them feel good but when their ministry contributes to the health of the Body of Christ" (p. 45).

Perichoresis and Teams

There is, in the community of God's self, no sense of dominating hierarchy. I agree with Miroslav Volf (1998) when he writes that "even if the Father is the source of the deity and accordingly sends the Son and the Spirit, he also gives everything to the Son and glorifies him, just as the Son also glorifies the Father and gives the reign over to the Father" (p. 217). Volf simply cannot find a connection between the communal nature of God and an ecclesiastical justification for hierarchical systems. Positioning himself apart from centrist Roman Catholic and Eastern Orthodox thinking on the Trinity, Volf believes that the "structure of trinitarian relations is characterized neither by a pyramidal dominance of the one (so Ratzinger) nor by a hierarchical bipolarity between the one and the many (so Zizioulas), but rather by a polycentric and symmetrical reciprocity of the many" (p. 217). This polycentric reciprocity is another way of describing the perichoresis of the persons of the Trinity.

All Christians are brought into fellowship with the triune God and are immersed in a sense of community distinct from the world's power systems. Volf applies trinitarian community to the entire community of God's people, observing that Jesus' priestly prayer brings all believers into "correspondence with the unity of the triune God (John 17:20; cf. 1 John 1:3)" (p. 218). On the basis of these texts, and 1 Corinthians, chapter 12, Volf concludes that "the symmetrical reciprocity of the relations of the trinitarian persons finds its correspondence in the image of the church in which *all* members serve one another with their specific gifts of the Spirit in imitation of the Lord and through the power of the Father. Like the divine person, they all stand in a relation of mutual giving and receiving" (p. 219).

The design of creation in Genesis, the life and ministry of Jesus, and the image of the triune God in perichoretic fellowship derived from Scripture all give strong grounding to a team-based church for the postmodern world.

Workplace Empowerment

In Search of Excellence, by Thomas Peters and Robert Waterman, Jr. (1982), represents for many a major shift in management thinking. In a clear and concise manner, Peters and Waterman framed the conversation for many books and research projects to follow. By taking a close look at what they defined as America's best-run companies, they came up with a set of eight basic principles to succeed. Three in particular relate to participatory ministry:

> Staying close to the customer—learning his preferences and catering to them
>
> Autonomy and entrepreneurship—breaking the corporation into small companies and encouraging them to think independently and competitively
>
> Productivity through people—creating in *all* employees the awareness that their best efforts are essential and that they will share in the rewards of the company's success [p. i; emphasis added]

The first principle—staying close to the customer to cater to his preferences—is generally discredited as an appropriate goal of the church. To think of church members as customers, for whom the church modifies its ministry in order to cater to them, smacks of becoming a consumer church. The concern is that the church will water down its radical message to make it more palatable to a consumer-oriented population. Examples of churches that have done just that are the high-profile television ministries that seem to do little in the way of forming community, fostering discipleship, or engaging in mission and instead pump a schmaltzy Christian message that does little more than entertain people and emotionally manipulate them to obtain financial contributions. But I wonder if we often retreat too far away from consumer satisfaction to a fortress of arrogance, if we say to people, in essence, "your needs and desires represent a threat to our righteousness." The emphasis for the church in responding to the larger social culture should not be, How can we give our members only what they want? That would constitute an abdication of the radical gospel message. We should, however, stay close to the customer for another reason. The church is constantly in need of learning how to communicate the Gospel effectively. We can stay close to our *constituents* in order to learn the language they speak, the symbols they are influenced by, the music that stirs them, the hopes and fears that drive them, and the hungers that obsess them. We can learn the vernacular of language and culture in order to communicate *the radical message of Jesus.* Because we are convinced that in the arena of real life, where real people live real struggles and issues, the

Spirit of God will take our message and transform broken lives, we should learn how to stay close to people so that we can know them and minister to them effectively and sensitively.

Here is a simple example: church leaders are correctly concerned about the quality and theological integrity of worship. They work hard, as they ought to, to conduct worship services that are meaningful, evoke praise and prayer, and lift up the worship of the people of God. But what they might not realize is that a portion of the church population is not present because the restrooms are filthy. Absent, in particular, are young parents who need a place to change their babies' diapers but find the restrooms so distressing that they fear for their infants' health. I find the concern of these parents valid. A form of caring is to provide a healthy environment for children. If this environment is not provided, the worship service will not be attended. The leadership team may never know about the condition of the restrooms if its members do not stay close to the people and hear their concerns.

A more serious example is the worship team that planned a series of services with the title, "Are You Ready for Jesus' Return? Services Focused on the End Times!" Meanwhile the congregation was reeling from the public disclosure that industrial pollutants had been the cause of the high number of terminal cancer cases in the community and church. Staying close to the people might have meant, in this case, designing worship services and other programs to deal with myriad issues from coping with terminal illness to working for justice in the community.

In relation to the second principle, autonomy and entrepreneurship, Peters and Waterman found that within the ranks of excellent corporations, *champions* were allowed to flourish. This is not always the case in organizational life: "Champions are pioneers, and pioneers get shot at. The companies that get the most from champions, therefore, are those that have rich support networks so their pioneers will flourish." This is something "so important it's hard to overstress," Peters and Waterman say. "No support systems, no champions. No champions, no innovations" (p. 211).

In the church environment such champions are found among the laity. They are the pioneers of relating faith to the business they work in, the home they manage, and the neighborhood they lie in. Ministry is unleashed when they are finally trusted with the responsibility of really being the ministers of the church and not just identified as such ministers on the cover of Sunday bulletins under a heading like, "Our church members are our ministers." I once heard of a minister who preached a strong sermon on the ministry of the laity and at the conclusion asked all those who wanted to serve in the church as lay ministers to come forward. More than a hundred made the trip, after which the minister leaned over and whispered to his associate, "What are we going to do with all these ushers!" Unleashed ministry is *real* ministry given back to the people.

Peters and Waterman's principle of productivity through people is also one churches can heed. Leo Bartel, vicar for social ministry in the Catholic diocese of Rockford, Illinois, calls church volunteers "unpaid staff" (Drucker, 1990, pp. 161–169). In other words, the employees of the church are all of us. We are employed by God to serve the Kingdom of God and exhibit it to the world. We do this not out of our own power but by leaning heavily upon the Spirit of God. We seek to live forth perichoretic community in the world and the responsibility for doing that— and the rewards of doing that—belong to the whole people of God. Our productivity is not measured in widgets but in service in the vineyard of the Lord. This makes it hard to measure our effectiveness with any sort of clarity, but we labor to do so nonetheless, because we are interested in knowing if we are communicating effectively in various contexts.

Peters and Waterman and many other business and organizational writers encourage leaders to keep close to employees, draw them into the life of the organization, and give them a share in it. For example, an article in *Fortune* magazine commented that a General Motors effort to bring "financial information down to the shop floor" and give workers a greater sense of "partnering" with GM in business "is a major step in bridging the gap between management and labor; *more than any other single act, it makes the goals explicit and the nature of the partnership concrete*" (Peters and Waterman, p. 267). The financial information informed workers of the plant's costs compared to profits. The workers could then see how their work measured up against financial goals. This kind of information sharing never happened before. Workers had been kept in the dark concerning the effectiveness of their labor, and "not even foremen would have been privy to such information at GM in the past."

Information sharing is a form of power sharing. It is a way of spreading out responsibility and drawing everyone into the effort that consumes the organization. Churches need to learn to share information and thereby spread out the responsibility for ministry to their whole memberships. Participatory management for us is not a trend or a cliché. It is a sacred task.

Examples of business and organizational reform that emphasize team-based approaches are being published weekly. Katzenbach and Smith (1994), for example, are among those who make the point that teams work best in today's cultural milieu. First, they argue, teams bring together complementary skills and experiences in a collaborative effort. Second, teams are flexible and quickly responsive to changing events and demands. Third, a social dimension (fellowship) is created in teams so that "team performance eventually becomes its own reward." And, fourth, "teams have more fun" (p. 18).

Postmodern organizations are moving toward participatory, team-based approaches because they work and they fit the cultural mind-set. Churches should become team based because it is the right thing to do theologically and biblically. The similarity between this reform and both corporate reforms and cultural changes in society should not prevent us from making the reform or from learning from our secular organizational counterparts. I suggest further that we in the church not only learn to do team-based ministry as well as companies use teams *but that we do it better, exhibiting our Kingdom values and mission*—so that, when Wal-Mart trains its sales teams, the trainer will say, "I want you to listen to our customers with the same concern and attention that churches show in listening to their people."

Building a Team-Based Church

Here are a number of practical ways to introduce and implement an empowering ministry with a team-based approach.

Begin with the Leader and the Leadership Team

All the chapters in Part Two have emphasized the importance of beginning with the leadership team to implement change. To build a meaningful community, the leadership team must model the attributes of perichoretic fellowship. I have also stated throughout that any meaningful change toward building community must have the support and endorsement of the principal leader. It is quite difficult and probably impossible to make needed changes when the principal leader does not support them. Once the leader and the leadership team become committed to implementing the ideas and concepts of reform, change can begin. If they are successful in creating an appealing model of Christian community in mission and ministry, it is likely to spread throughout the congregation. People care about how the leaders get along and function together. Their own families and work environments are full of dysfunctional relationships and conflict. People want to know if the church leaders can learn to work together, and if they can, their model will have a powerful influence throughout the church and even the town or city at large. It is that powerful and influential.

Work Out in Concentric Circles

Churches, like most organizations, can be illustrated structurally with the leadership team at the center and the subsequent levels spreading outward in concentric circles. Once the leadership team has formed its team community, the next group that needs to reform itself is the next level of leaders: in most churches this level will consist of the elders, deacons, parish council, or board of directors.

I observed this method of working outward from the team center unfold in a remarkable fellowship called Spirit of Peace Roman Catholic Community, in Longmont, Colorado. I was pastor at the time (1983 to 1987) of Westview Presbyterian Church, which housed the buildingless fellowship. The vision for a team-based model of ministry came from fellowship's founder-priest, Daniel Flaherty, under the auspices of the late James Casey, who was then archbishop of the diocese of Denver. "Dan," as he insisted on being called, formed the paid staff into a team, along the same lines I have suggested here. The team, made up entirely of unordained people, administered the worship and programs of the fellowship. Within the larger fellowship, it encouraged the formation of *small communities* (teams), each with a dozen or so families engaged in various forms of prayer, Bible study, and outreach. All the functions of the fellowship were carried out by laypeople except for those requiring a priest. In those situations, either Flaherty or some other priest was called in to perform the priestly office. The emphasis was not on the individual priest but upon the rite. Thus, although Flaherty was the founder-organizer and ensured the fellowship was connected to the diocese and had what it needed to be a church, the fellowship was led by teams. I marveled at its success as its growth quickly outpaced ours. I further observed a joy and delight in the people (staff and volunteers) who ran the programs, conducted the worship, grew spiritually in their small communities, and saw the fellowship grow into a strong mission-oriented church in that region of Colorado.

Dorothy Feehan, Sister of Charity of the Blessed Virgin Mary, was on the leadership team at that time and continues in that role today. She once told me that

> At Spirit of Peace we seek to live out our deep call in baptism that Christians are to take the responsibility for living the words of the Gospel. The team model uses a consensus style of leadership where each person takes responsibility for decision making. In the team model, people also take more responsibility for their spiritual devel-

opment. They ask, "What is God calling me to do in my own unique environment; a personal environment that is in communion with the church at large? In addition, how does living out the Gospel in my personal environment, and in the communion of the church, work to change the world?" For example, we chose the name Spirit of Peace because we identified violence as a major problem in the world. We hope, through our small communities, to change the world.

The Spirit of Peace success began with the vision of the founder-leader who developed a leadership team that lived out team-based ministry. From there, other leaders were drawn into forming ministry teams and small communities that became the heart and soul of a highly effective Christian fellowship.

Immerse Everyone in Biblical Examples of Team Ministry

We can use biblical and theological material to influence leaders and congregation toward an enabling, permission-giving, team-based approach. (For example, teams can use the material in this book as a study guide, and they can also find helpful materials in the other works referenced here.) We can preach on the scriptural passages. We can teach team ministry in classes and board meeting settings. We can make team ministry a central theme of our ministries.

When I served at Covenant Presbyterian Church, my ministry became synonymous with the phrase, "Every Member in Ministry." I was constantly talking about it, teaching it, preaching it, telling stories about it, and in any way I could, influencing the leadership and the church toward an enabling style of ministry. Over the years, the concept took root.

Build the Organization Around Empowering Teams

We should restructure the organization of our churches in such a way that enabling, team-based ministry is reinforced and taught repeatedly over years. For example, at Covenant Presbyterian my staff and I changed all the session committees into teams, and all the primary ministry teams (responsible for the principal ministry areas in the church) met on one night. First, the team leaders met at 6 P.M. to facilitate communication and coordination of the several ministry areas. Then, at 6:45, all the team members (150 to 200 of them) met in the sanctuary for worship. We sang, prayed, and read Scripture. At 7 P.M., I gave what amounted to a vision-casting talk. It lasted only about ten minutes, but it praised the efforts of the teams, recognized our progress, emphasized the importance of team ministry, and encouraged all the teams to continue to enable church members to participate in our many ministries. At about 7:15, each team went to a separate area in the church facility to work and plan, occasionally walking over to another team to collaborate with it on some ministry.

In other words, we designed our structure and our ways of doing things to reinforce team-based, participatory ministry that viewed each member as a minister of the Gospel.

Sabotage Power Controllers with the Truth

We should, paradoxically, sabotage those who try to work against a collaborative, team-based approach. We can do this by telling the truth. I have stressed that political sabotage on teams is contrary to perichoretic fellowship. But foiling plans to seize power by revealing them to the light is what I call *honest sabotage* and fits our model of love. The people who will most resist a collaborative, enabling team-based model are those who like having the power themselves. Certain controlling personalities will be convinced that the leadership of the church—the elders, deacons, leadership team, and so forth—is not capable of running the church. The way to deal with those who try to sabotage team ministry is to expose their efforts during the open, and honest team discussion that is part of the reform process. The efforts will then be either quickly disbanded in the light of the revelation or be confronted by the leaders of the church and their power abated. In my experience, those who work against the team model because it threatens their own sense of power and authority are often sincere people who have not yet realized the spiritual benefits of a collaborative approach. Over time, and with sensitive pastoring, these people can become strong allies. Only rarely have I come across people considerably more resistant and hardened, who, when it is obvious the church is moving toward an empowering model and they cannot fight it, leave the congregation.

Use Team Stories, Symbols, Language, and Models

We should tell stories of effective teams wherever we go. One of my favorites concerns a baseball team, the 1969 Mets. They came from the basement in the league standings in 1968, with no previously recognized superstars, to win the 1969 world series. How did this happen? Teamwork. Effective teamwork goes far beyond what a superstar can do. Another favorite story of mine comes from Kouzes and Posner's *The Leadership*

Challenge (1995) and concerns Arlene Blum, who put together an all-female climbing team to go to the top of Annapurna I in the Himalayan Mountains. Team members had their vision firmly in mind: "If we succeeded, we would be the first Americans to climb Annapurna and the first American women to reach eight thousand meters (26,200 feet)" (p. 92). But in order to accomplish their feat, they had to overcome barriers ("women aren't strong enough") and pull together as a team.

We should tell not only stories like these but also stories that come out of our congregations. We can make heroes out of those who collaborate to do teamlike work in the church. We can use Rick Warren's method of mentioning heroes and heroines in sermons and even (by prearrangement with them) introduce them and have them tell their own stories.

Change Meeting Configurations

If we are going to encourage a more collaborative, enabling environment, we have to change our configurations for meetings. How we set up meetings and conduct meetings communicates what we value. This is true not only for the principal leader or pastor, but for all those who lead or moderate committees, teams, discussion groups, and other meetings in the church.

Years ago I was sent by my denomination to report to a session about the work of the denomination. The pastor and his clerk sat at a head table. The twenty-four elders present sat in chairs that faced the head table. The chairs were arranged five across in five rows, configured like the seats in a movie theater. All eyes were on the pastor-moderator who led the discussion and answered most of the questions raised. He was set up as the authority and the one responsible for the organization, the one with all the answers.

Configuration speaks volumes. Change it to reflect an enabling style. Meet in a circle. Although the moderator is certainly a principal player in moderating the discussion, we should be sure to spread out power and responsibility so that more and more people are the answer-tellers.

In one church I pastored, an inactive elder was convinced I was solely responsible for changing *his* church, and he campaigned to the nominating committee to be put on the session. The nominating committee asked me if I minded. I said it was up to them and that it would not bother me. The elder ended up on the session, and at his first meeting he grilled me with a list of criticisms about the church and its ministries. I did not respond to any of them because I had positioned (configured) the meeting so I was not the only one responsible for the organization. In fact, I had used my responsibility as pastor-leader to give away responsibility. We all sat in a circle, and as he fired off each criticism at me, I pointed him to the person who was responsible for that particular area of service. He quickly realized that his criticisms were aimed not at me but his friends sitting beside him—fellow elders—who took offense at his tone of voice and sharp attacks. "We welcome your suggestions, Jeb," they replied, "but we're just like you, trying to do our best with what we have." Remarkably, over a year's time, Jeb became one of our best elders, realizing that he was part of a larger team taking responsibility for the ministries of the church.

Make Team Building More Than Technique: Make It a Lifestyle

Moving chairs around and renaming committees teams is not enough. Team building has to become a spiritual discipline for the principal leadership team. The individuals on the team have to want it, believe in it, and live it. Furthermore, they have to model it. This means listening, respecting differing viewpoints, drawing out ideas that seem bizarre but may be God's word to the church, surrendering one's own way, and developing the art and skill of consensus building. It means giving up the need to control for the greater good of seeing God in control through the work of the church and collaborative leadership.

I have equated enabling the ministry of the laity with developing ministry teams, cells, and small communities because it is my continuing experience that empowering the people, releasing their gifts and passions and baptism callings, is best done in a team-based environment. Although churches may support some ministries that are performed by sole individuals, I believe that the need for accountability almost always requires that people be empowered for ministry in groups rather than as individuals out on their own.

9

THE LEARNING TEAM

EFFECTIVE MINISTRY teams are ever growing and open to new discoveries. They have an insatiable appetite to learn. The learning team is not satisfied with its present state but seeks to grow spiritually and to know more about doing ministry in more effective and meaningful ways.

Jesus called us to be more than church members; he called us to be disciples. Churches must raise up a new generation of disciples who have learned to work together in collaborative teams. These teams are growth oriented. Team members encourage one another's spiritual growth and walk with Jesus Christ. They hold each other accountable. They desire to be houses of love that take the sense of community seriously. Learning teams are spiritually growing teams.

From trial and error, learning teams build a depository of learnings that help them be more effective in ministry. They take risks in innovation. They allow for failure because they know that failure is a form of learning and growing.

Teams must learn and, based on their learning, change and innovate because the world is changing quickly. In order to minister to people in the flux of such change, the church needs to encourage ministry teams that will try a variety of ways to communicate. Language and cultural identifiers are not static, and the church needs to keep up on change in order to speak the language of the people. The Gospel is best told in the vernacular, and that vocabulary keeps changing.

Ministry teams must be learning teams because they seek to be communicators of the Gospel in the world. When I was in high school, my youth group pastor had a sticker in his office that said, "Leaders Must Be Readers." Today, they must be readers, perceivers, sensers, listeners, observers, and Internet surfers. We are better missionaries to the postmodern world when we know its language and culture.

Effective church teams, then, will find ways constantly to grow. They know they cannot remain static; however, their growth is not frantic. It is rather a spiritual discipline, a way of life. They find ways to keep current and thrive on that learning. They cultivate a joy in learning a new rhythm and moving to it because they see the Spirit at work in their efforts to reach out with the Gospel.

Effective church teams find beauty and wonder in new discoveries. And they delight in living them out.

Continuing Education in Appleton

The Apple Hill Church hardly resembles the First Church of Appleton described in Chapter Three. Over the years, it has come a long way. Although the leadership team, consisting of staff, initiated much of the change in the early years, the Apple Core Team, consisting of elders, took on more and more responsibility for the ministries of the church as time went on. The leadership team members became team consultants, helping other teams get off the ground. They mastered forms of training and the discipling of others. The Apple Hill Church also became a teaching church, helping other church leaders and congregations make important changes to adjust to a postmodern world. They entered into a dialogue with peer churches, sharing discoveries and learning from one another. Peer learning became a principal form of continuing education for church leaders. Delegations were sent out from the Apple Hill Church to other congregations both to share what the Apple Hill Church had learned and to learn new ways of thinking about and doing ministry. Denominational lines seemed blurred. Theological differences, though important, could in many cases be set aside in order for people to learn how to reach out more effectively in mission and ministry.

As team consultants and trainers, the leadership team must keep growing. There is always a lot to learn about God, about how church works, about how to relate the Gospel to culture, and about what it means to be a faithful disciple of the Lord Jesus Christ. Furthermore, the Apple Hill leadership team has learned that its effectiveness in ministry has resulted in a more complex organization that has a perpetual amount of *chaos* associated with it. Learning how to manage the chaos and remain in good spirits in a sprawling organization can be challenging—and immensely fulfilling. The fulfillment keeps coming from the same place: the transformed lives, the renewed hope for the hopeless, the mission endeavors that result in better communities, the social issues worked through to a new level of justice, the examples of new love shared, the life-stealing compulsions replaced by a Spirit-driven love for God—the list is endless and it is energizing. This is what brings the Apple Hill team members back each working morning to their team building: the evidence of the Spirit of God in their church and their love, forged through difficulty, experienced in the team body.

The Learning Conversation

Learning took place at the Apple Hill Church primarily through dialogue between the church teams and culture and between the teams and other churches' experiences. Although the Apple Hill Church is fictitious, its experiences nonetheless represent typical true situations.

My most important learning experiences have come through peer conversations. Talking out loud to a colleague seems to form thoughts and experiences in my mind that express my present dilemmas and joys. The give-and-take in conversation tests ideas, sharpens thoughts, and illustrates concepts with real-life narratives and stories that embody those concepts. These experiences plant learning in the context of reality.

Physicist Werner Heisenberg (1971) discusses this same relationship in telling of the conversations he had over a lifetime with Pauli, Einstein, Bohr, and other scientific pioneers. These conversations, he says, literally produced many of the great theories associated with these names. And Peter Senge (1990) finds that "Heisenberg's conversations, recalled in vivid detail and emotion, illustrate the staggering potential of collaborative learning—that collectively, we can be more insightful, more intelligent than we can possibly be individually. The IQ of the team can, potentially, be much greater than the IQ of the individuals" (p. 239).

The Apple Hill leadership team initiated learning forums where people from other teams, both inside and outside the congregation, shared their experiences. These experiences became a narrative of learning. The networks of relationships created by these forums became learning networks. And in the process of sharing lessons, lives were shared. Community was created.

Growing Up

Christians are forgiven people who are justified through faith by God's saving grace. There is nothing we can do to earn or deserve our salvation. It is a free gift from God. "For the wages of sin is death, but the free gift of God is eternal life in Christ Jesus our Lord" (Rom. 6:23).

Forgiven and justified before God, the Christian life is one of growth. Scripture refers to Christian growth as *sanctification*. For example, the Shorter Catechism of the *Westminster Confession*, with questions and answers derived from Scripture, gives this response to the question, "What is sanctification?" "Sanctification is the work of God's free grace, whereby we are renewed in the whole man after the image of God, and are enabled more and more to die unto sin and live unto righteousness." Having been redeemed by Christ, we now desire to live for Christ in the world. And while we live in this world, we are being changed more and more into the image of God through growth in the Spirit: "You were taught to put away your former way of life, your old self, corrupt and deluded by its lusts, and to be renewed in the spirit of your minds, and to clothe yourselves with the new self, created according to the likeness of God in true righteousness and holiness" (Eph. 22–24).

Sanctification involves not only personal spiritual growth but also the living of our baptism in the world. Recall Dorothy Feehan's statement that "at Spirit of Peace we seek to live out our deep call in baptism that Christians are to take the responsibility for living the words of the Gospel." One of the primary scriptures supporting this way of living is found in Romans, "Therefore we have been buried with him by baptism into death, so that, just as Christ was raised from the dead by the glory of the Father, so we too might walk in newness of life" (6:4). We are emerging in this newness of life, living our baptism, our calling, in the world.

Christians are called, then, to be growing people. We are being sanctified by the Spirit, meaning that God is working within us to renew and re-create us. We are undergoing a process of change and growth.

To the church at Ephesus, Paul wrote about this process of change and growth in terms of growing up:

> The gifts [Jesus] gave were that some would be apostles, some prophets, some evangelists, some pastors and teachers, to equip the saints for the work of ministry, for building up the body of Christ, until all of us come to the unity of the faith and of the knowledge of the Son of God, *to maturity, to the measure of the full stature of Christ. We must no longer be children,* tossed to and fro and blown about by every wind of doctrine, by people's trickery, by their craftiness in deceitful scheming. But speaking the truth in love, *we must grow up in every way into him who is the head, into Christ,* from whom the whole body, joined and knit together by every ligament with which it is equipped, as each part is working properly, promotes the body's growth in building itself up in love [Eph. 4:11–16; emphasis added].

Growing up spiritually includes developing our personal spiritual disciplines. Team members must be prayerful, Bible-immersed people who seek ways to live out their individual callings in the places God has planted them.

Growing up spiritually includes developing our corporate spiritual disciplines. As Paul teaches us, we have been graced with gifts to be used for the common good in the Church of Jesus Christ. The combined use of these gifts in Christian fellowship and worship draw us to the "unity of the faith and of the knowledge of the Son of God, to maturity, to the measure of the full stature of Christ."

Growing up spiritually includes living our faith by doing the good works of God in the world. We do these things not to deserve God's favor but in gratitude for all God has done for us. These works are evidence of our faith. "So faith by itself, if it has no *works,* is dead. But someone will say, 'You have faith and I have works.' Show me your faith apart from your works, and I by my works will show you my faith" (James 2:17–18).

The doing of good works includes our efforts at mission and ministry. These tasks and spiritual disciplines are not ways to obtain favor from God. They are rather an offering back to God for all God has done for us. The pursuit of our cause, our mission from God, is a joyful response to grace. And this mission involves growth and development. As we live out our faith, we are being matured in our faith in the Spirit. We are growing up.

Growing up spiritually means giving away our faith. Jesus spoke about surrendering life to find it. One of the true evidences of mature faith is whether or not it is being lived in mission and given away. Mature fruit creates the seed for new growth. Howard Butt Jr. (1996) writes about this spreading of faith through teams that resemble the fellowship of the Trinity: "Jesus' initial twelve person team, . . . [t]he one working team Christ started with in the days of his flesh now multiplies, divides, and explodes in the days of his Spirit, becoming not just one, but *many* working teams, decentralized" (p. 161). Mature teams propagate themselves. They share what they have learned so that others may sprout and grow.

In his discussion of the doctrine of sanctification in relation to Ephesians, chapter 4, theologian Shirley Guthrie (1994) asks, "Are you *growing?* Have you settled down comfortably with the growth you have behind you, or are you willing to keep up the painful, constant struggle to keep on growing? Is your Christian life an attempt simply to hold on to what you think you have already achieved in your relation to God and other people? Or are you willing to risk what you have already learned and accomplished to explore new and more complete ways of loving God and other people?" (p. 337).

Perichoresis and Growth

When we are baptized "in the name of the Father, and of the Son and of the Holy Spirit," we are immediately in communion with God and the church. We are made one with Christ and made part of the body of Christ. But this baptism is not static. It involves us in creative movement, as I have suggested earlier. Ushered into the presence of the triune God, we are being shaped by the "potter's hand" (Jer. 18:6) to live out the Kingdom in all of God's creation. Baptism and mission are intimately tied together. Jesus gave his disciples a mission of baptizing others (Matt. 28:18–20). Our baptism is not a passive splashing to make us at peace with God. It is a commissioning that draws us into the peace-filled fellowship of God and then sends us into the fray to live out God's peace in the world.

We do not, however, live the commissioning (the cause) of God as completed persons. Rather, as people under construction by the Spirit, we seek always to learn and grow. Through prayer, meditation on the Scriptures, church fellowship and dialogue, and experience in culture and creation, we seek to learn and grow, to become more and more in the likeness of God. I cannot emphasize enough that being made in the likeness of God is not a private religious enterprise. It is a communal activity that involves a holy conversation between the Christian and God, the Christian and other Christians, and the church and the surrounding culture.

Workplace Learning

In *The Fifth Discipline: The Art and Practice of the Learning Organization* (1990), Peter Senge challenged my thinking in many ways about developing a learning organization, and his work has had considerable application in the business world. Teaching corporate managers to be learners might sound like a good corporate strategy for encouraging the development of better products to increase the bottom line, but I found Senge's work to go far beyond helping organizations keep up with culture in order to sell more. Rather, he approaches learning as foundational to the human enterprise and key to developing meaningful, growth-filled places of labor.

For example, Senge makes the observation that children grow by expanding their awareness. Children sense external forces and how they are related to them. They learn that they are part of a greater reality, which they influence in a variety of ways. Children sense, for example, that they can get warm by moving closer to Mommy or Daddy. Though the environment may be chilly, they learn that they can do something to be warmer. Their sense of reality is constantly changing as they take in new information about it, react to it in terms of their own needs, and influence it as needed.

A child experiences a progression of discovery about reality and his role in it. "At each stage in this progression, there will be corresponding adjustments in his internal pictures of reality, which will steadily change to incorporate more of the feedback from his actions to the conditions in his life" (p. 170). And there is a parallel between this process of discovery and the learning organization: "The learning process of the young child provides a beautiful metaphor for the learning challenge faced by us all: to continually expand our awareness and understanding, to see more and more of the interdependencies between actions and our reality, to see more and more of our connectedness to the world around us" (p. 170).

The learning enterprise as Senge describes it fits well into the model presented here of the learning team in the church as the discovering team that seeks constantly to be expanding its awareness, to grow more and more in the likeness of God, and to reach out to the culture beyond the church with the Gospel.

No Longer Newtonian

Stephanie Marshall (1997) insists that organizations today must change their concepts about learning. Marshall, the founding executive director of the Illinois Mathematics and Science Academy in Aurora, Illinois, believes that today's so-called crisis in education arises primarily from our recent shift in how we conceive the world (what I have been calling the shift to postmodernism). She argues that education is hanging on to old paradigms that no longer fit our new worldview, and that "inherent in the old mental models are three mechanistic metaphors that have historically contextualized our view of schooling and learning: universe as a clock, brain as computer, and learning as tabula rasa (blank slate)" (p. 179). Education has been held hostage by these mechanistic metaphors. The result has been that "we constructed and operated our [mechanistic] schools as we understood our world, and this produced iatrogenic and learning-disabled institutions that have suppressed reflective thought, creativity, and the innate and inexhaustible human capacity for lifelong growth. The unexamined application of Newtonian laws to complex adaptive social systems diminished our capacity for continuous growth and change because it diminished our capacity to 'grow' the individual and collective intelligence, energy, spirit, and hope of the whole system" (p. 180).

Marshall believes we need to "create a learning culture that provides a forum for risk, novelty, experimentation, and challenge and that redirects and personalizes learning. We must create learning communities for learners of all ages that can give power, time, and voice to their inquiry and their creativity." These communities could be governed by principles of *learning,* not *schooling.* For example, these communities could be

- Personalized, flexible, and coherent (learning is connected to real-life issues)
- Internally and externally networked and not bounded by physical, geographic, or temporal space
- Invitational, with students engaged in meaningful research and serious inquiry
- Accountable to the learner to provide adaptive instructional environments
- Rich in information and learning experiences for all learners
- Open to emergent and generative knowledge
- Self-organized around core principles, beliefs, and a shared and mutually creative purpose
- Intergenerational in the configuration of learning experience
- Flexible, diverse, and innovative
- Interconnected and collaborative, fostering interorganizational linkages
- Engaged in authentic dialogue with members of the internal and external community
- Focused on inquiry, complex cognition, problem finding, and problem resolution
- Committed to increasing what David Perkins, in *outsmarting IQ,* calls the "learnable intelligences" of every individual
- Comfortable with ambiguity and paradox
- Playful
- Trusting

- Responsible
- Loving [pp. 183–184]

Marshall believes that twenty-first century learning communities based on the such principles must be viewed as "dynamic, adaptive, self-organizing systems, not only capable but inherently designed to renew themselves and to grow and change" (p. 184). This organic (rather than mechanistic) model of the learning community fits the biblical image of the body of Christ for perichoretic team ministry. Learning teams are living teams, not machines, that thrive and grow and develop, under the guidance of the Holy Spirit, to become all that God calls them to be. Churches must change their views of organization, moving away from bureaucratic, highly mechanized models, and must embrace a more biblically and theologically sound model that is more relational and dynamic.

Building Learning Teams

The following are practical ways churches can build learning teams. Learning communities, such as teams, can become very strong entities of Christian discipleship and mission, making a profound influence on both the church population and the town or city in which they are located.

Cultivate Spiritual Discipline

Teams must be growing spiritually. Techniques for effectiveness cannot substitute for vital faith. Prayer, Bible study, and a sense of acting on one's personal mission must be essential habits of every team member. Churches must provide for the spiritual growth and discipling of all their members, especially those on ministry teams.

Mike Foss pastors the sprawling, growing Prince of Peace Lutheran Church in Burnsville, Minneapolis. The vitality and enthusiasm of the lay ministry of this exciting congregation are founded in prayer. "In the congregation," Foss told me, "there has emerged a deeper need to walk with Jesus Christ, evidenced by a tremendous prayer ministry that is growing and growing. People are needing specific guidance in living their faith: not in a way that is 'do this' and 'do that,' but in a way that respects people and allows them to be honest about their problems in spiritual growth."

After Foss came to Prince of Peace and encouraged the staff to care for one another and foster each other's spiritual growth, his administrative assistant surprised him by telling him, "No pastor has ever cared about my spiritual life before." But team members must care about each other's spiritual life. In fact, they must be able to count on each other to be prayerful, spiritually disciplined people.

Model Learning

Just as the principal leader must model the other team attributes I have discussed, he or she must model spiritual and professional growth. Most churches provide continuing education allowances for their leaders. These funds must never go unused. The leader should not only model personal spiritual and ministerial growth and development but should encourage the leadership team and other teams to engage in endeavors that help them grow. The leader arranges discussions of failures and mistakes as learning moments during team meetings, and a person making a mistake can be rewarded and honored for taking a risk. The leader also reflects on personal failures or mistakes and what he or she has learned from them. Time is provided for continuing education during team meetings. Special retreats and learning events are scheduled. These events go beyond the traditional teacher-student format. They are interactive, engaging, and hands-on experiences that expand awareness and skill.

Principal leaders of all teams, not just the leadership team, must network with their counterparts in other churches to engage in growth conversations. My own peer network includes pastors from all over the country who serve churches similar to the one I serve. Theologically, they range from conservative to liberal. They are also denominationally diverse, representing most of the mainline traditions and many independent and new paradigm churches. I look to meet pastors who are entrepreneurial, experimenting with new concepts and models, willing to take risks, and dealing with problems similar to the ones I face.

Develop Team Networks

Teams too must develop peer networks that engage in ongoing conversations about ministry. These conversations exchange more than words. Networked teams visit one another, experience worship in each other's churches, experiment with new ideas and ministries, and then discuss their experiences with one another.

In this way, teams go beyond the continuing education event that sponsors only the good thinker to the event that sponsors both thinkers and *doers*. As Marshall suggests through her principles of new era education, learning is more than attending a lecture that imparts knowledge to the passive student. Those who learn today must be "connected to real-life issues" (ministry), "internally and externally networked and not bounded by physical, geographic, or temporal space," "open to emergent and generative knowledge," and "engaged in authentic dialogue with members of the internal and external community." Simply attending a lecture titled, say, "The Various Apocalyptic Interpretations of the Revelation of John," is not enough. However, attending this lecture *and* discussing with peers the effect of apocalyptic thinking on the church today and how it effects ministry in real life is valuable.

Years ago, Covenant Presbyterian Church hired a director of children's ministry. My staff and I recognized in her the gifts for becoming a leader in children's ministry, but she lacked experience in the larger church context. So we sent her to various educational and training events around the country that did far more than put her in a chair and feed her information. In addition to being given good insights and stages-of-learning information, she *experienced* what children experience in interactive curricula. She moved around discovery stations, engaged in dramas to illustrate biblical stories, sampled educational computer programs and emerged as a highly trained, competent team leader for a children's program involving hundreds of children. In her training experiences, she met education team leaders from around the country, and they are now her peer network. Her training included more than theory and was not classroom bound; it focused on hands-on, interactive, age-appropriate learning experiences, and it continues to do so.

Train People for Ministry

Our continuing education and training must be intentional and must include all people in ministry. We must make sure that all our teams have clear and specific training events and that every team member is required to attend training and continuing education events.

When Peter Drucker (1990) interviewed Leo Bartel, vicar for social ministry of the Catholic Diocese of Rockford, Illinois, he noticed that under Bartel's leadership the diocese had grown in size and scope of services offered yet had fewer priests than before. "How did you accomplish this Miracle of the Loaves and Fishes?" Drucker asked. Bartel replied that volunteers had taken up the slack, commenting that "the volunteers of the past were 'helpers.' Our volunteers now are 'colleagues.' In fact, we shouldn't even talk of 'volunteers' anymore; they are really 'unpaid staff'" (p. 161).

Bartel's unpaid staff, or team members, however, need training because of their added responsibilities. They must constantly be growing. Bartel reports: "The formal training in the Lay Leadership Program runs over a two-year period. We have seven courses, which range from scripture to communications to evangelization to theology. This program is intended to take people who have shown ability and give them the kind of training that will make them effective, give them a sense of being qualified" (p. 163).

On-the-job training is also important, over and above the formal training program. Bartel comments, "We are very careful to develop opportunities for individuals to share their difficulties as well as their triumphs with each other. We give them opportunities to deepen in themselves and in each other the sense of how important the things are that they are doing" (p. 165).

Be Mosaic

Teams must read profusely. We should choose our reading from lots of different sources, and that reading should be *mosaic* rather than *linear*. It might move, for example, from the Bible to *Rolling Stone* to *Theology Today,* taking in also the *New York Times* and a sampling of *Wired*. This reading forms a mosaic, or collage, of different and varying impressions rather than following a straight line of similarity. We can listen to CDs that are being produced for the younger generations to be aware of emerging music, but we can also notice how listening to a classical symphony can give our minds a sense of harmony, a sense of interconnecting themes and movements. Country-western ballads tell stories and teach us how to communicate experiential narratives. For years, I was critical of myself for watching television shows. Now I realize that over the years I have derived an intuitive sense of communication from being an audience for media productions. We can watch television, go to the movies and theaters, and ask ourselves: Is this communication effective? How are narrative, irony, paradox, satire, comedy, drama, and creative tension being used? What makes for communication that is both effective and honest? What are the communication techniques that feel manipulative and coercive, and what must the church do to avoid using them? Our media, communications, and worship teams should be engaged in learning conversations to define appropriate and inappropriate communications for the church. How do we move beyond religious entertainment in worship to sacred drama that evokes discipleship? We must fill our minds and our experience with a diverse set of impressions and learnings that make us and our teams more effective in a postmodern world.

Avoid Arrogance and Complacency

Churches that experience strong growth and develop a healthy ministry, equipping and deepening the faith of their people, can then become arrogant and complacent. How easy it would be for a church like Apple Hill, sending out its now successful leadership team to teach its form of ministry, to fall into the trap of arrogance and complacency. Ministry is dynamic and complex. What seems to work today may not tomorrow. Leaders must be vigilant against behaviors and attitudes that can quickly undermine the ministry, such as becoming proud. Teams must also constantly be retooling for new challenges and opportunities. We cannot afford the luxury of complacency in a world that hungers so much for the church to live its faith. And we certainly must avoid taking credit due to the Spirit of God! Furthermore, whereas businesses have an easy way of determining corporate success (the profit margin), the church must avoid depending too much on quantitative measures and remember that the *effectiveness* of Jesus' ministry culminated when he was rejected by the crowd and nailed to a cross. In light of this sacrificial success, we must humbly seek out ways that go beyond numbers and figures to evaluate the effectiveness of our ministry.

Make Heroes out of Those Who Fail

In learning as in other attributes, celebrate failures and publicize mistakes in a way that creates heroes. If we ridicule or punish the person who makes a mistake in attempting to do ministry, we will quickly snuff out innovation. Instead, we can conduct a worship service now and then on the learnings that come from failure. We can have laypeople tell their stories of learning from mistakes, and create an oral tradition of learning from failure. We can use other communication media in the church to report failures, as a way of rewarding attempted innovation.

Years ago I was asked by the Austin, Texas, United Way to serve on an advisory board for a new information and referral network linking government social service agencies, nonprofit organizations, and religious groups in the city with those in need of their services. I was asked to be on the board because I had failed earlier to create such a network myself. At my first board meeting, I introduced myself by saying, "Hello. I'm George Cladis, and I've been asked to serve on this board because I am a failure." I paused because people were giggling. "I failed to do what we are now aspiring to do, and I am here because I learned a few things from my failure that can help us succeed." I did not regard my failure as something to be embarrassed about. It contained useful experience, and today in Austin there is First Call for Help, an excellent information and referral network sponsored by the United Way. I like to think that my earlier failures contributed in some small part to First Call for Help's success.

Finally, consider this important admonition from Leo Bartel: "The fact is . . . if people are properly motivated . . . developing competence becomes part of their very need. My biggest difficulty in asking people to serve is that they are painfully aware of their lack of experience and lack of preparation. If we can provide them with that, they're eager to learn" (Drucker, 1990, p. 164).

A WORD OF ENCOURAGEMENT

THE PERICHORETIC MODEL of Christian fellowship presented in these chapters can be the basis of a powerful leadership team for churches and organizations ministering in a postmodern world. Here are a few final reflections for leaders and teams now beginning the practical steps that will develop this exciting way of doing ministry.

Be Patient

Ministry is difficult. There is a complex web of church and community constituents that constantly demand attention. There is a never-ending string of needs. How easy it is for leaders to be consumed in organizational maintenance and never get to the proactive things needed to move ahead.

The rewards of developing team ministry along the lines suggested in this book are tremendous. Be patient, and take the time necessary to forge ahead. Plan your steps. Work diligently with your fellow leaders. Remember that ministry takes time. Persuasion is an art that cannot be rushed. Be tenacious in your efforts to communicate the benefits of collaboration, and then take the time necessary to work the steps toward forging a powerful fellowship of leaders.

Learn from Failure

Team-based ministry is highly relational. Most of us can think of several failures we have experienced in relationships. Make those failures your teachers. Learn from them what you need to know about your style of ministry and about the kinds of people you do and do not get along with, and reflect on what you need from coworkers to feel safe and secure. Process your failures in such a way that you can talk freely about them and demonstrate their educational benefits. Make the living narrative of your life a reflection on how God has led you, molded you, and formed you into the person God has for a specific role. Do not be afraid to be honest about both your successes and failures.

Recognize That There Are No Perfect Fellowships

Attempting to build church teams on a model based on the perichoretic community of the persons of God is quite an ambitious goal. But so are most goals we are about in the Church of Jesus Christ. Although the picture of God's self-fellowship is a noble and worthy image to work toward, we must remember that we are not God, and we are prone toward very human emotions such as fear, jealousy, envy, pride, and arrogance, to name a few. When your fellowship fails to live up to its high standards—and it will from time to time—do not be too discouraged. Learn and grow from the experience and move on. I am convinced that following the guidelines suggested in this book will build strong theologically and culturally appropriate teams, but they will not be perfect teams. Our life together is difficult and stressful. There is nothing more difficult than managing relationships. There is also nothing more fruitful or meaningful, particularly when we have occasion to celebrate the ways in which our fellowship has lived out God's plan and purpose. These are thrilling and rewarding moments!

Sometimes I am introduced at conferences as an "expert in team relationships." I am happy to share what I have learned. But I am also a bit uncomfortable with the role of team expert. In a way, it is like being touted as an expert in parenting. I would never dream of calling myself an expert in parenting when I am constantly struggling in my own life with how to be a better father to my teenage children. In the same way, who can be an expert at team ministry? Relationships are difficult, and some of them tax us to our limits. There are no experts in these waters—only experienced mariners who have traveled the same seas and who can cite the likely places of shipwreck, who have a healthy regard (and some fear) for the power of the currents, and who can thus offer *humble* guidance for navigating them. This is my role, and I am constantly learning new things about these oceans for which I have developed a deep respect.

Be of Strong Faith

I close this book with the same admonition I introduced in the Preface. The model and practical steps suggested here are no substitute for vibrant, vital faith. Focus there first. In all I have suggested, I have assumed that leaders desire to be disciples of the Lord Jesus Christ. In addition, I have assumed that those interested in implementing team leadership know the importance of prayer and Scripture reading. I can give suggestions for ways to live out your faith. I cannot give the faith itself. That is between you, God, and your team.

I hope, however, I have succeeded in communicating that this model is a way to live out your faith. I have rarely been more enthused than I have been seeing this model work so well in the congregations I have served and in those with which I have consulted. And one of the reasons why it works so well is because its participants can readily see how it is grounded in Scripture and Christian theology. To live it is to feel as if one is on a sacred quest.

Blessings to you on your own sacred journey into team ministry.

TWO EXAMPLES OF STAFF COVENANTS

THIS RESOURCE CONTAINS two examples of staff leadership team covenants. The first is from Noroton Presbyterian Church in Darien, Connecticut, where I now serve as pastor. It is an example of a short covenant. The second is from Covenant Presbyterian Church in Austin, Texas, where I previously served as pastor. This covenant is a longer example, containing significant theological and liturgical grounding. Use these examples to launch you into your own innovative thinking about negotiating and writing team covenants.

NOROTON PRESBYTERIAN CHURCH OF DARIEN, CONNECTICUT

STAFF TEAM COVENANT

Serving NPC into the twenty-first century, and seeking to be a brilliant beacon of Christ's light in the world, we, the staff of Noroton Presbyterian turn to the power and mystery of the Trinity as our covenantal anchor! We boldly, joyfully affirm God in three persons, the holy embodiment of encircling love: intimate, equal, interconnected! As a trusting and collaborative team we are seeking to discover, experience, and pass on the revealed, felt presence of God—Father, Son, Holy Spirit; Creator, Redeemer, Sustainer! From within this circle of Love, then, we come to discern and fulfill, by grace, God's purposes, God's visions, and mission for our lives, for Noroton, and for the "body of Christ" universal. In our covenantal model, we try to imitate the Godhead, three in one, who creates and blesses (Father), who redeems and restores (Son), who encircles and empowers (Holy Spirit), who unites and loves!

Ephesians 4:1–3
I, therefore, the prisoner of the Lord, beg you to lead a life worthy of the calling to which you have been called, with all humility and gentleness, with patience, bearing with one another in love, making every effort to maintain the unity of the Spirit in the bond of peace.

Ephesians 4:15,16
Speaking the truth in love, we must grow up in every way all things into him who is the head—into Christ—from whom the whole body, joined and knit together by every ligament with which it is equipped, as each part is working properly, promotes the body's growth in building itself up in love.

Ephesians 5:1,2
Therefore, be imitators of God as beloved children and live in love, as Christ loved us and gave himself up for us, a fragrant offering and sacrifice to God.

We, the staff of NPC, desiring to be faithful to Christ in our relationship with each other, and to model the love and unity as demonstrated by the Father, Son, and Holy Spirit, do covenant to the following:

- Seek to appreciate and live out our God-given individual blessings with a sense of awe.

- Intentionally encourage and bless one another.

- Draw out each other's gifts while making the weaknesses irrelevant.

- Put an emphasis on self-grace and grace with one another rather than perfection.

- Speak well of fellow staff to others.

- Forgive ourselves and one another.

- Work through problems rather than bury issues.

- Disagree openly, avoiding triangulation and speaking unkindly of others.

- View all ministries as an interlinking circle; no beginning, no ending, no one more important than the other.

- Like the potter and the clay, be willing to be molded and changed.

- Communicate, both to each other and to the congregation.

- Make time for fellowship, worship, and prayer together.

- Respect, honor, and trust each other.

COVENANT PRESBYTERIAN CHURCH
OF AUSTIN, TEXAS

STAFF TEAM COVENANT

Prelude

Jesus said to her, "Woman, believe me, the hour is coming when you will worship the Father neither on this mountain nor in Jerusalem. You worship what you do not know; we worship what we know, for salvation is from the Jews. But the hour is coming, and is now here, when the true worshipers will worship the Father in spirit and truth, for the Father seeks such as these to worship him. God is spirit, and those who worship him must worship in spirit and truth."

—John 4:21–24

Worship is at the very center of the life of the Church of Jesus Christ and the followers of the Savior. From the fountain of Christian experience in worship flows the Life and Presence of Christ into all of who we are and where we go.

In worship,

we recognize God calling us together as a people to be in covenant with the Almighty and with one another.

In worship,

we give praise and adoration to the One who has rescued us from sin and death and brought us up, out of the grave, into new life and light.

In worship,

we acknowledge who is the Creator and who is the creature and our need for forgiveness.

In worship,

we hear the ancient testimony and the word proclaimed that we might encounter the Word afresh for the transformation of our lives and the world.

In worship,

we respond to the grace, love, and call of God with our lives, offered in humble devotion to be of service to the reign of God.

In worship,

we baptize into the covenant, commune with God and one another, and offer our lives as a living sacrifice in response to the gift of God in Jesus Christ.

In worship,

we are sent out in mission to take the worship, love, and peace of God into a dark and broken world.

Worship, then, is not an hour-long experience on Sunday morning of religious entertainment in music and speech; rather, who and what we are orbits constantly around the life and devotion and communion that emanates from continuous worship.

The Christian lives daily in the midst of a grand reverberation of the chorus that surrounds the throne of God:

> *Holy, Holy, Holy Lord,*
> *God of power and might.*
> *Heaven and earth are full of your glory.*
> *Hosanna in the highest!*
>
> *Blessed is he who comes in the name of the Lord.*
> *Hosanna in the Highest!*

In worship, we see the symbols of faith and hear the message of hope. We take this worship, this music of God's heart, into the world. Worship and daily living are intimately linked, like partners in a dance, where God is the choreographer.

> At an office coffee pot, a Hispanic man from east Austin pours a cup of coffee and looks for sugar. A white man from west Austin opens a cupboard, sees the sugar, passes it over. Smiles are exchanged. A "thank you" and a "you're wel-come." *Take. Eat. This is my body broken for you. Do this in remembrance of me. The bread is passed and shared. Black, brown, yellow, red hands all sharing the bread. The chorus is heard in every land. The words repeated. The bread shared. Community created.* Coffee shared today. More of our lives tomorrow?

A close dance of worship pressed dearly to life. Joined. Moving to the music of God.

A woman heading a large corporation sees an opportunity to gain an edge over a competing company. But the action is illegal. No one will notice, she thinks. It will not be seen by anyone. Hidden from view. She can get away with it. *Carolyn, I baptize you in the name of the Father, the Son and the Holy Spirit. [The anointing with oil.] You are marked! You belong to Jesus! From death you have been bought and set free to serve God alone!* The temptation is difficult to fight off. *Off comes the world. Go forth now clothed in Christ!* She decides not to do it.

The symbols and liturgies of worship taken into the world, echoing with the song of eternal praise, a rhythm of life with Christ that is taken out of stained-glass, pipe-organed sanctuaries and into the world where you and I live!

The Covenant

The Staff of Covenant Presbyterian Church, Austin, Texas, are determined to take the worship of God and live it in our faith community.

This *Staff Covenant* represents our conviction that benedictions, indeed all of worship, can be lived out in the community of the staff of Covenant Church:

> *Go in peace.*
> *Serve one another.*
> *Walk humbly with thy God.*

We began the development of the *Staff Covenant* in the summer of 1995 by taking approximately two hours a week for six weeks to talk about Christian worship (particularly *Reformed* worship) and how it touched our lives in community with another. We talked about ourselves, our needs, our past and present work in the church, our hopes for the future, and our failures and successes in relationships. We discussed our individual Myers-Briggs types and how they seem to function with other types. We talked about our different ways of perceiving the world, our gender differences, and varying backgrounds. We prayed and discussed theologically how our work might be joined together in harmony to give praise and adoration to God in Christian service.

Those who developed this covenant also have strong convictions that the effectiveness of church ministry is in large part dependent upon the good working relations among the church staff. This is a great responsibility that should not be taken lightly or left to unspoken assumptions but made clear in a working covenant as we have here designed. We hope that our covenant might be a model to other leadership in our congregation of different people joined in Christ living worship out in community and mission. We hope that our covenant might also serve as an example to other church staffs of how such a project can be done. We want our experience to be informative to others who want to take worship into the world and into the church office!

After a total of ten hours of discussion spread over a month's time centered on the relationship of Reformed worship to staff relationships and how we uniquely fit together as a church staff, Pastor George Cladis wrote a draft covenant based on the conversations. A draft copy of the *Staff Covenant* was presented at a staff retreat in September 1995 for review. The program staff had been the primary contributors to the covenant up to this point. The retreat involved the support staff as well. All the staff were divided into small groups to discuss the covenant and then brought back together into a whole for further discussion. Suggestions for changes were made. A second draft copy was submitted to all the staff at the following staff meeting. The *Staff Covenant* as amended was adopted by the group as a working covenant for our church staff.

The decision to include the program staff first in the covenant process and the support staff later was made for three reasons.

1. It was practically difficult to include all the staff in the many hours of meetings to develop the draft copy of the *Staff Covenant*.

2. The program staff form the leadership nucleus of the congregation. They are, furthermore, more experienced in church staff relationships and were able to draw on a wealth of past experience and personal and spiritual maturity essential for the early steps of the process.

3. The program staff are theologically trained and more able to reflect on the nature of our staff relationships in terms of Reformed worship. The program staff's education and experience were important for the early drafting of the *Staff Covenant*.

The Session of the congregation has an extensive *Personnel Handbook* for employees and pastors of the church, which includes personnel processes and forms similar to those found in companies and corporations. The desire of the staff was to forge a *spiritual* and *theological* covenant that would form the basis for our working relationship together and complement the *Personnel Handbook*. As one of our Lutheran support staff members described it, "The *Personnel Handbook* is the letter of the law while the *Staff Covenant* is the spirit of the law."

Furthermore, staff felt that the broad brushstrokes of how we want to be in relationship with each other (for example, "we will be truth-tellers") rather than specific behaviors (for example, "we will wait patiently in line at the photocopier") was preferred.

It is important to note that a final staff conversation about the *Staff Covenant* focused on the expressed feelings of inability fully to live out this covenant. It was recognized that though these words challenge us to a high calling, and though we will likely fail to live it perfectly or completely, it is nonetheless a model of how we desire to work together and we are committed to living it out, as enabled by God's grace, in our church staff community.

> *The Covenant Presbyterian Church Staff Team*
>
> *September 1995*

Praise and Preparation

But Moses said to the people, "Do not be afraid, stand firm, and see the deliverance that the lord will accomplish for you today; for the Egyptians whom you see today you shall never see again. The lord will fight for you, and you have only to keep still. . . ."

Then Moses stretched out his hand over the sea. The lord drove the sea back by a strong east wind all night, and turned the sea into dry land; and the waters were divided. The Israelites went into the sea on dry ground, the waters forming a wall for them on their right and on their left.

—Exod. 14:13–14,21–22

Now about eight days after these sayings Jesus took with him Peter and John and James, and went up on the mountain to pray. And while he was praying, the appearance of his face changed, and his clothes became dazzling white. Suddenly they saw two men, Moses and Elijah, talking to him. They appeared in glory and were speaking of his departure [Gk: exodon], which he was about to accomplish at Jerusalem.

—Luke 9:28–31

Theological Introduction

God initiates the covenant. God opens the door, invites, welcomes, calls us into fellowship, embraces at the entrance, makes us new through the waters, sets the table, breaks the bread, pours the wine, and makes promises to us. The most profound promise of covenant love was spoken to Moses by the Lord from the burning bush on Mount Horeb. To Moses' first objection, God replied: "I am with you." Throughout history, God has repeated this covenant promise, "I am with you." The epitome of such love and promise came in Jesus, the Son, who was Emmanuel, God with us.

God makes this happen. We are undeserving of such love. The Lord in great love and affection for creation, reaches to us and initiates the renewed relationship.

Worship, then, begins with this affirmation: God calls us together and, by grace, initiates a relationship of covenant love and *withness*. We enter by grace, are made new by grace, restored by grace, and are brought into fellowship and covenant by grace. God opened the waters for the Hebrews to pass through to the mountain of the covenant of God. So, too, God opens the way to fellowship with the Lord and one another. In Jesus Christ, a new exodus has happened, to make a way from God to us forged by the love and grace of God.

This new exodus is profoundly and mysteriously represented in the Sacrament of Baptism in which we are called, affirmed, named, washed, marked, and sent out to serve.

Both Baptism and the early movement of Reformed worship involve the confession of sin and the renouncing of evil. In our confession, we experience God's pardon and are set loose again to praise and adore the Redeemer and Reconciler!

Application

The Covenant Staff take this first movement of worship and understand that we are called into a relationship with Christ, both personally and professionally, that is initiated by the Creator God and dependent upon God's grace. Our ministry is not our own, it belongs to God. In Baptism, we take off the world and put on Christ. In ministry, we take off the things which divide us and put on Christ and rely upon God's grace to love as we have been loved.

We desire our work together to be fulfilling and meaningful. We want to see the Holy Spirit at work through our combined labors. Our work is an expression of our faith, and consequently, we desire our labor to be God centered. We imagine our work to be productive but not overly burdensome; a joyous labor not leading to intense burnout; an experience that lifts our spirits rather than crushes our initiative. As God joyously hurled into place the stars and planets and called them good, so we work with our hands, minds, and hearts to create in love and devotion. We want our creations to be in partnership with God's creation. The cultivation of hobbies, interests, and relationships allow for refreshment of our spirit and mind to be at work for Christ in the church.

The Call to Worship is followed by acts of praise and adoration. The Covenant Staff are called into ministry by Christ and we find vital meaning and satisfaction in offering our labor together as praise and adoration to God.

> When we lead worship, it is out of joy and gratitude.
>
> When we orchestrate singing and musical instruments, it is in adoration of the Covenant Maker.
>
> When we teach and instruct, lead youth and children, reach out with tender care, or serve with hammers and saws in mission, it is a living praise.

The Confession of Sin reminds us that we are prone to fears and jealousy. The Covenant Staff covenant to work at recognizing our anxiety as we experience it. Name it before God. And share it with one another when appropriate. We understand that a spark of enmity between us can ignite a conflagration within the church. Our commitment is to do the hard thing and share our problems with one another. As malice brewed in the heart of Cain, God warned, "sin is lurking at the door; its desire is for you, but you must master it" (Gen. 4:7). We must master the difficult feelings within us and between us before they can do severe damage in our relationships and in the church.

The Covenant Staff then seek to build trust among the staff, all of whom are in partnership with God and one another in ministry. God finds us, calls us, cleanses us, renews us, and then commissions us to live out grace in community. Shared grace builds mutual trust. Out of gratitude, we seek to reflect the grace, honesty, and truth of the One who called us together and covenants to be with us.

The truth we face about ourselves is sometimes difficult to encounter. Yet we are obliged to be truth-tellers with one another as God is with us.

We recognize that temptation often occurs in types resembling those that came from the devil to Jesus (Matt. 4:1–11). When it comes to desires for money and pleasures, we recognize that we do not live by bread alone but by the Word of God. When tempted to do risky behaviors or those things which might bring reproach upon the ministry, we seek not to put the Lord to test. And when we would be lured to use power inappropriately rather than as servant leaders, we will work to remember that we bow down and worship God alone. The Covenant Staff work for just and fair relationships. Things such as job descriptions, tasks, salaries, and other parts of working relationships will be worked out together with the appropriate Session leaders to ensure harmony, fairness, and collegiality among the staff.

God does not hold grudges. Forgiven, our iniquities are also forgotten. As God has been for us, we also seek to be for one another, living out mercy and grace with each other, aware that we will suffer conflict from time to time, but also aware of our hope for renewal and reconciliation in the God of the cross and empty tomb.

Assured of God's pardon, and living grace upon grace with one another, we lift our arms before God and give adoration and praise:

> *Glory be to the Father,*
> *And to the Son,*
> *And to the Holy Ghost!*
> *As it was in the beginning,*
> *Is now and ever shall be.*
> *World without end.*
> *Amen.*

We Encounter the Word of God

On the day the tabernacle was set up, the cloud covered the tabernacle, the tent of the covenant; and from evening until morning it was over the tabernacle, having the appearance of fire.

—Num. 9:15

In the beginning was the Word, and the Word was with God, and the Word was God. He was in the beginning with God. All things came into being through him, and without him not one thing came into being. What has come into being in him was life, and the life was the light of all people. The light shines in the darkness, and the darkness did not overcome it.

There was a man sent from God, whose name was John. He came as a witness to testify to the light, so that all might believe through him. He himself was not the light, but he came to testify to the light. The true light, which enlightens everyone, was coming into the world.

He was in the world, and the world came into being through him; yet the world did not know him. He came to what was his own, and his own people did not accept him. But to all who received him, who believed in his name, he gave power to become children of God, who were born, not of blood or of the will of the flesh or of the will of man, but of God.

And the Word became flesh and lived among us, and we have seen his glory, the glory as of a father's only son, full of grace and truth.

—John 1:1–14

But when Christ came as a high priest of the good things that have come, then through the greater and perfect tent* (not made with hands, that is, not of this creation), he entered once for all into the Holy Place, not with the blood of goats and calves, but with his own blood, thus obtaining eternal redemption.

—Heb. 9:11–12

Theological Introduction

Emmanuel. God with us. The God who tabernacled with us in the wilderness came to dwell with us in person. The Word of God, Jesus Christ, is God with us who lived among us and showed us the Father. The tabernacle of the Old Testament and the One who tabernacled with us in the New Testament were both tabernacles of the covenant: the promise of God to be with us and to stay in relationship with us. The covenant relationship is made possible through the blood of the perfect sacrifice, Jesus Christ.

In the worship of God we encounter afresh the Word of God. We pray for the illumination of the Spirit of God, read from the Bible, listen to the Scriptures in music, and proclaim the Message of the Good News of Jesus Christ. In our encounter with the Word, the Message comes into our hearts with consolation and conviction for the day in which we live. As the Word made flesh taught, healed, forgave, stirred, confronted, consoled, and renewed, so the Word encountered comes to us as a congregation and as individuals with such force and power. We are deeply touched. We are moved to focus again on Christ. And our most immediate response again is praise!

Application

The Covenant Staff agree that we cannot be with the people of the church we serve unless we are also being with the God who tabernacles with us. Our strength to give and minister comes from the Spirit who dwells within. We agree individually to take time to encounter the Word in prayer, Scripture study, and service. We want to listen for God and experience the Lord

---

**NRSV translation note: Also translated as* tabernacle.

in our lives. It is our conviction that our own wisdom and strength is not enough; we depend upon the Lord and feed from God's hand.

The Covenant Staff also realize that we often encounter the Word through other people. We desire to cultivate relationships that guide and direct us spiritually. We strive to make the fellowship of the Covenant Staff such that we encounter God in one another. We will look for the face of Christ in each other, render ourselves accountable to one another, pray for each other and our needs, and hold each other up in high esteem as those whom God created, cherishes, redeems, and in whom tabernacles the Spirit of God.

God in Jesus Christ *was and is present to us*. And so we pledge ourselves to be present to one another, spending the time we need to build quality relationships.

God in Jesus Christ *listens to us*. We pledge ourselves to a listening ministry, hearing each other's perspectives and respect one another's opinions.

God in Jesus Christ *prays for us*. We pledge ourselves to a prayerful ministry, remembering one another and our individual needs and ministries to God.

God in Jesus Christ *breaks bread with us*. We pledge ourselves to a ministry where we plan times of recreation and meals with one another to refresh and renew our spirits.

God in Jesus Christ *heals us*. We pledge ourselves to a ministry where we are sensitive to each other's wounds and hurts, are compassionate, and join with God in a healing response.

God in Jesus Christ *was and is a living proclamation of God's grace and Word for us*. We desire our working relationships to be living proclamations of God's grace and call to obedience to conform to the mind of Christ.

Respect will mark our relationships as together we seek God's Word to us for today.

Our encounter with the Word kindles praise and fans it wildly.

> *Joy to the world! the Lord is come:*
> *Let earth receive her King;*
> *Let every heart prepare him room,*
> *And heaven and nature sing,*
> *And heaven and nature sing,*
> *And heaven, and heaven and nature sing.*

—Isaac Watts (1719)

Our Response to the Word

While they were eating, Jesus took a loaf of bread, and after blessing it he broke it, gave it to the disciples, and said, "Take, eat; this is my body." Then he took a cup, and after giving thanks he gave it to them, saying, "Drink from it, all of you; for this is my blood of the covenant, which is poured out for many for the forgiveness of sins. I tell you, I will never again drink of this fruit of the vine until that day when I drink it new with you in my Father's kingdom."

When they had sung the hymn, they went out to the Mount of Olives.

—Matt. 26:26–30

I appeal to you therefore, brothers and sisters, by the mercies of God, to present your bodies as a living sacrifice, holy and acceptable to God, which is your spiritual worship.

—Rom. 12:1

Theological Introduction: Sacrament of the Lord's Supper

The Word proclaimed leads now to the Word made visible in the Sacrament of the Lord's Supper. It is a holy transaction. God's gifts to us of body and cup; our response with the gifts of our lives. The giving to us of the Self of God solicits our grateful response of the gifts of our selves back to God.

We begin with the invitation. The God who initiated the covenant with us in love now invites us to the feast where we are united with Christ and with one another.

> *Friends, this is the joyful feast of the people of God!*
> *They will come from east and west,*
> *and from north and south,*
> *and sit at table in the kingdom of God.*

Application

The Covenant Staff understand that our staff members come from all over. We are from San Francisco, Richmond, Chicago, Miami, Austin, Baton Rouge, and many other places. We are men and women. We have different family heritages representing many places from around the world.

We are all invited to the table. There is no Greek or Jew, no distinction between men and women, and no slave or free. We are all invited and served by Christ.

The Covenant Staff are determined not to allow our differences in places of origin, gender, or other distinctions to determine the value of the individual. We are all equally cherished at the table. No one of us is more favored of God. We treat each other as full members of the household of God.

Theological Introduction: Amnanesis

The Prayer of the Great Thanksgiving, or Eucharistic Prayer, is one of gratitude. We commune in joy and thanksgiving for the gift of God to us in Jesus Christ who has won for us our salvation and enabled our fellowship with God.

The Eucharistic Prayer begins with the *amnanesis,* or "remembering," of God's salvific acts. By remembering them, we reappropriate them for today and we acknowledge that our lives and services continue the arena of God's redemptive and reconciling work on earth.

> *The Lord be with you.*
>> And also with you.
> *Lift up your hearts.*
>> We lift them up to the Lord.
> *Let us give thanks to the Lord our God.*
>> It is right to give our thanks and praise.
> *It is truly right and our greatest joy*
> *to give you thanks and praise,*
> *O Lord our God, creator and ruler of the universe.*
> *In your wisdom, you make all things*
> *and sustain them by your power.*
> *You formed us in your image,*
> *setting us in this world to love and to serve you,*
> *and to live in peace with your whole creation,*
> *but we turned from you,*
> *leaving sin and death to reign.*
> *Still you loved us and sought us.*
> *In Christ your grace defeated death*
> *and opened the way to eternal life.*

We give you thanks that the Lord Jesus,
on the night before he died,
took bread,
and after giving thanks to you,
he broke it, and gave it to his disciples, saying:
Take, eat.
This is my body, given for you.
Do this in remembrance of me.

In the same way he took the cup, saying:
This cup is the new covenant sealed in my blood,
shed for you for the forgiveness of sins.
Whenever you drink it,
do this in remembrance of me.

Application

The Covenant Staff seek to work as living reminders of what God has done and thereby give witness to what God can do. When we dream impossible dreams together in staff meetings, we remember Moses standing at the sea when God did the impossible. When we are faced with injustices and disobedience to God's will, we feel the indignation of the prophets. When we are crushed and feeling hopeless, we remember the cross and the resurrection. When we are opposed and persecuted for following the Master, we remember the example of the Apostles and early church leaders. As living reminders of what God has done, we point to a living God who still works miracles, heals, redeems, and breaks down walls.

Theological Introduction: Epiclesis

The *epiclesis* is the giving of the Spirit which blesses the elements and, in our communion, forms us into the body of Christ. The giving of the Spirit is the mysterious miracle of God and is a divine action we cannot control or conjure up but freely is offered by God to us as we obediently do what God commands in the breaking of the bread.

Application

No one member of the staff contributes more than another to the spiritual growth and development of the congregation. While some staff members may be more *productive,* only God gives the life. We bring to the table the bread and wine. God does the miracle. We offer to God together, as the Covenant Staff, our labors and offerings. We trust God to bless the efforts and give the life!

Theological Introduction: The Sharing of Bread and Cup

We are fed at the table and made one with one another and God through the giving of God's gifts. The Spirit of God makes us the body of Christ on earth. As God has been given to us in the Sacrament, we now unite to give our lives back to God and to one another in service to Christ in the world.

Application

The Covenant Staff remember 1 Corinthians, chapter 12. We are different parts of the body but the same Spirit unites us. We need each other. An interdependence exists in our work of praise we offer to God. God has brought us together for a common good. We value the diverse gifts represented in the different people of the staff.

We Take Our Worship into the World

And you became imitators of us and of the Lord, for in spite of persecution you received the word with joy inspired by the Holy Spirit, so that you became an example to all the believers in Macedonia and in Achaia. For the word of the Lord has sounded forth from you not only in Macedonia and Achaia, but in every place your faith in God has become known, so that we have no need to speak about it.

—1 Thess. 1:6–8

I appeal to you therefore, brothers and sisters, by the mercies of God, to present your bodies as a living sacrifice, holy and acceptable to God, which is your spiritual worship. Do not be conformed to this world, but be transformed by the renewing of your minds, so that you may discern what is the will of God—what is good and acceptable and perfect.

—Rom. 12:1–2

Theological Introduction: The Hymn of Praise and the Charge and Benediction

Praise begins and ends our prayers and worship. We gather to praise and we exit with songs of praise in our hearts and minds. Praise saves us from excessive seriousness about the business of life. We are not in control. God is the Sovereign One. Praise cures our minds of excessive anxiety. The story of God has a good ending. Praise reminds us that we are the creature and God is the Creator! Praise permeates our service; it paves our exit from the sanctuary of church building and leads us into the sanctuary of God's world. Hymns led to the crumbling of prison walls in Philippi (Acts 16:25–26). Hymns lead us to be bearers of the liberating Word of God in Jesus Christ.

The charge gives us marching orders. We are a people with a purpose. Our worship does not end now but is carried by the body of Christ into the world. As partners with God in mission, we are employed by the Lord to reclaim the world for God. Our lives and gifts have been dedicated for this purpose.

We are not alone in our work. The triune God—Father, Son, and Holy Spirit—is promised to be with us, enabling us to accomplish what God has set out for us to do. We are the sowers of the seed of faith. God gives the seed and grants the life. Without God's benediction, our work is empty and dead. The promises of God to tabernacle with us in the world lead us to be bold in mission and proclamation of the one true God.

Application

The Covenant Staff work with large hands upon them. For those of us ordained to an office in the church, the weight of the tradition passed to us is a responsibility to do and be what God and the church have set forth in Scripture and polity. For those not ordained, the hands of God nonetheless weigh upon us as a blessing and an equipping to serve as God has called us to do.

The Covenant Staff recognize that our work is directed to those who live in the world. We serve the congregation who are sent forth to be God's people in difficult places. We pledge ourselves to serve them and aid them in their service to Christ in the world. We recognize that our ministry is not to give orders to members but to encourage them in their ministries. The members of Covenant Church are the ministers who bring the Gospel to the world. Our work is to help enable and educate that ministry. And we seek to do that with praise!

Postlude

The music streams out the doors. The song sends us out. It is the song of God's grace and charge to be the people of God in the world.

Other church staffs have had noble ideas of community and communion that have, nonetheless, become only words without substance. Will our covenant follow such a fate? Will our good words and exalted notions be just a song in the wind. Or will this covenant be a strong melody frequently in our minds and hearts, percolating through all we are and do, and making a difference in who we are and the witness we bear to Christ?

The Covenant Staff agree that much rests on our ability to live this covenant for each other and for Christ. It is our commitment and praise to live it as God's grace enables.

To the King of the ages, immortal, invisible, the only God, be honor and glory forever and ever. Amen.

—1 Tim. 1:17

REFERENCES

Anderson, B. W. *Understanding the Old Testament*. (4th ed.) Englewood Cliffs, N.J.: Prentice Hall, 1986.

Anderson, W. T. "What's Going On Here?" In W. T. Anderson (ed.), *The Truth About the Truth: De-Confusing and Re-Constructing the Postmodern World*. New York: Putnam, 1995a.

Anderson, W. T. (ed.). *The Truth About the Truth: De-Confusing and Re-Constructing the Postmodern World*. New York: Putnam, 1995b.

Barna, G. *The Power of Vision*. Ventura, Calif.: Regal, 1992.

Barth, K. *Church Dogmatics*. Vol. 2: *The Doctrine of God: Part 1*. (G. W. Bromiley and T. F. Torrance, eds.; T.H.L. Parker, W. B. Johnston, H. Knight, and J.L.M. Haire, trans.). Edinburgh: Clark, 1957.

Bolman, L., and Deal, T. *Leading with Soul: An Uncommon Journey of Spirit*. San Francisco: Jossey-Bass, 1995.

Bonhoeffer, D. *Life Together*. (J. W. Doberstein, trans.). New York: Harper-Collins, 1954.

Boss, W. R. "Trust and Managerial Problem Solving Revisited." *Group and Organization Studies*, 1978, *3*(3), 331–342.

Briskin, A. *The Stirring of Soul in the Workplace*. San Francisco: Jossey-Bass, 1996.

Brueggemann, W. *Genesis: Interpretation*. (J. L. Mays, ed.). Louisville, Ky.: Westminster Press/John Knox Press, 1982.

Buford, B. *Halftime*. Grand Rapids, Mich.: Zondervan, 1997.

Butt, H. E., Jr. *Renewing America's Soul*. New York: Continuum, 1996.

Carroll, J. W. *As One with Authority*. Louisville, Ky.: Westminster Press/John Knox Press, 1991.

Collins, J. C., and Porras, J. I. *Built to Last: Successful Habits of Visionary Companies*. New York: HarperCollins, 1994.

Connellan, T. *Inside the Magic Kingdom*. Austin, Tex.: Bard Press, 1996.

Covey, S. *The Seven Habits of Highly Effective People*. New York: Fireside, 1990.

Deal, T., and Kennedy, A. *Corporate Cultures*. Reading, Mass.: Addison-Wesley, 1982.

De Pree, M. *Leadership Is an Art*. New York: Dell, 1989.

De Pree, M. *Leadership Jazz*. New York: Doubleday, 1992.

Drucker, P. *The New Realities*. New York: HarperCollins, 1989.

Drucker, P. *Managing the Non-Profit Organization*. New York: HarperCollins, 1990.

Easum, W. M. *Sacred Cows Make Gourmet Burgers*. Nashville, Tenn.: Abingdon Press, 1995.

Fowler, J. W. *Stages of Faith*. New York: HarperCollins, 1981.

Freiberg, K., and Freiberg, J. *Nuts! Southwest Airlines' Crazy Recipe for Business and Personal Success*. Austin, Tex.: Bard Press, 1996.

Friedman, E. H. *Generation to Generation: Family Process in Church and Synagogue*. New York: Guilford Press, 1985.

Greek-English Lexicon: An Intermediate Greek-English Lexicon Founded upon the Seventh Edition of Liddell and Scott's Greek-English Lexicon. Oxford: Clarendon Press, 1968.

Guthrie, S. *Christian Doctrine*. (Rev. ed.) Louisville, Ky.: Westminster Press/John Knox Press, 1994.

Hammer, M., and Champy, J. *Reengineering the Corporation*. New York: HarperCollins, 1993.

Hanson, P. D. *The People Called: The Growth of Community in the Bible*. San Francisco: Harper San Francisco, 1986.

Hayes, R. *First Corinthians: Interpretation*. Louisville, Ky.: Westminster Press/John Knox Press, 1997.

Heisenberg, W. *Physics and Beyond: Encounters and Conversations*. New York: HarperCollins, 1971.

Hoffman, L. A. *The Art of Public Prayer*. Washington, D.C.: Pastoral Press, 1988.

Hopewell, J. F. *Congregation: Stories and Structures*. Minneapolis: Augsburg Fortress Press, 1987.

Kanter, R. M. "Restoring People to the Heart of the Organization of the Future." In F. Hesselbein, M. Goldsmith, and R. Beckhard (eds.), *The Organization of the Future*. San Francisco: Jossey-Bass, 1997.

Katzenbach, J. R., and Smith, D. K. *The Wisdom of Teams*. New York: Harper-Business, 1994.

Kouzes, J. M., and Posner, B. Z. *The Leadership Challenge*. San Francisco: Jossey-Bass, 1995.

Kouzes, J. M., and Posner, B. Z. "Seven Lessons for Leading the Voyage to the Future." In F. Hesselbein, M. Goldsmith, and R. Beckhard (eds.), *The Leader of the Future*. San Francisco: Jossey-Bass, 1996.

Marshall, S. P. "Creating Sustainable Learning Communities for the Twenty-First Century." In F. Hesselbein, M. Goldsmith, and R. Beckhard (eds.), *The Organization of the Future*. San Francisco: Jossey-Bass, 1997.

Miller, D. M. *Reinventing American Protestantism: Christianity in the New Millennium.* Berkeley: University of California Press, 1997.

Newbigin, L. *The Gospel in a Pluralist Society.* Grand Rapids, Mich.: Eerdmans, 1989.

Nouwen, H. *Behold the Beauty of the Lord: Praying with Icons.* Notre Dame, Ind.: Ave Maria Press, 1987.

Ouspensky, L., and Lossky, V. *The Meaning of Icons.* Crestwood, N.Y.: St. Vladimir's Seminary Press, 1982.

Peters, T. J., and Waterman, R. H., Jr. *In Search of Excellence.* New York: Warner Books, 1982.

Russell, L. M. *Church in the Round.* Louisville, Ky.: Westminster Press/John Knox Press, 1993.

Schwarz, R. M. *The Skilled Facilitator: Practical Wisdom for Developing Effective Groups.* San Francisco: Jossey-Bass, 1994.

Senge, P. *The Fifth Discipline: The Art and Practice of the Learning Organization.* New York: Doubleday, 1990.

Slaughter, M. *Spiritual Entrepreneurs.* Nashville, Tenn.: Abingdon Press, 1994.

Slaughter, M. *Out on the Edge: A Wake-Up Call for Church Leaders on the Edge of the Media Reformation.* Nashville, Tenn.: Abingdon Press, 1997.

United Presbyterian Church in the United States of America. *The Book of Common Worship.* Philadelphia: United Presbyterian Church in the United States of America, 1946.

Volf, M. *After Our Likeness: The Church as the Image of the Trinity.* Grand Rapids, Mich.: Eerdmans, 1998.

Warren, R. *The Purpose Driven Church.* Grand Rapids, Mich.: Zondervan, 1995.

Wheatley, M. *Leadership and the New Science.* San Francisco: Berrett-Koehler, 1992.

Wren, B. "God is One, Unique and Holy." In *Faith Renewed.* Carol Stream, Ill.: Hope Publishing Co.

INDEX

A

Accountability: advantages to creating, 104; in collaboration, 102–105
After Our Likeness: The Church as the Image of the Trinity (Volf), 113
Amdahl Corporation, 95
Anderson, B. W., 35–36
Anderson, W. T., 18
Appel, E., 39

B

Barna, G., 56
Bartel, L., 134, 151–152, 154
Barth, K., 53
Baugh, K., 101–102
Bellesi, D., 50, 61–62, 64, 120
Blume, A., 139
Body of Christ: as parish model, 91–92; in postmodern age, 129–131; and team ministry, 91–92
Bolman, L., 24
Bonhoffer, D., 47
Book of Exodus, 4, 36, 68
Book of Genesis, 14, 69–70, 111, 129, 130, 131
Book of Revelation, 70
Boss, W. R., 116
Briskin, A., 24
Brueggemann, W., 129–130
Buber, M., 2
Buford, B., 75
Butt, H., Jr., 145

C

Calvary Chapel, 123
Calvinist movement, 83
Carroll, J. W., 21, 22, 27
Casey, J., 136
Cell teams, 124–128
Central Christian Church (Las Vegas, Nevada), 39
Champy, J., 20, 28
Chaplaincy model, 124
Church Dogmatics (Barth), 53
Church leadership teams: as collaborative team, 13–14; as covenanting team, 10–11; as culture creating team, 12–13; as empowering team, 15; as learning team, 15–16; seven attributes of, 10–16; as trusting team, 14–15; as visionary team, 11–12
Church maintenance, 106
Church in the Round (Russell), 5
Church team formation: and church in the round, 10–16; and circle dance model, 4–6; and master images, 3–4; and ministry teams in the postmodern world, 7–10, 31; and perichoretic Trinity, 4–6, 31–32; and round table leadership, 5, 6; and Rublev icon, 6–7, 8
Circle dance, 4–6, 93
Coast Hills Community Church (Aliso Viejo, California), 50, 61–62, 120
Collaboration: and body of Christ as team ministry, 91–92; and collaborative teams, 97–106; and community,

88–90; definition of, 89; and perichoretic collaboration, 92–94; and
team play, 91; and the workplace,
94–97

Collaborative teams: building of,
97–106; and generic church maintenance, 97–98; and identification
of dysfunction, 103–105; and passion, 98–99; and sharing of common philosophy, 99–102; and team
accountability, 102–105; and time,
106

Collins, J. C., 56, 73

Community of Joy (Glendale, Arizona), 121

Community Presbyterian Church
(Danville, California), 59–60

Congregation, 89

Connellan, T., 74–75

Constituency, 132–135

Corinthians, Epistle to, 5, 92, 93, 131

Covenant Presbyterian Church
(Austin, Texas), 40, 84, 137,
162–177

Covenanting leaders: commitment of,
41–42; importance of, 39–40

Covenanting teams: building of,
41–47; and commitment of team
leader, 31–42; and covenanting
God, 34–37; and covenanting leaders, 39–40; and distribution, 46;
and frequent reviews, 45; and
God's house of love, 34–35; and
graciousness, 47; honesty and self-
disclosure in, 43; and human communities reflecting house of love,
36–37; and Mosaic covenant,
35–36; and orientation of new
team members, 45–46; and sin,
43–44; sufficient time for, 42–43;
and team houses of love, 37; and
workplace covenants, 37–38

Covey, S., 24

Crosby, F., 83

Crosno, J., 79–80

Cultural environment. *See* Postmodern
culture

Culture-creating: and creation of
materials, symbols, and rituals,
68–69; and culture-creating god,
69–71; and going beyond generic,
67–68; and perichoretic culture,
71–72; and teams, 76–87; and
workplace culture creators, 72–76

Culture-creating teams: building of,
76–87; and communication,
82–83; and cultural diversity,
85–86; and elimination of competing cultures, 76–77; existing culture
as springboard for change in,
79–80; and group character,
77–78; language, liturgy, symbols,
history, traditions, customs, and
slogans in, 80–82; and making
heroes and heroines, 79; and
media, 86–87; and music, 83–85

Cultural diversity, 85–86

D

Davis, C., 98–99

De Pree, M., 20, 25, 37–38, 95

Deal, T., 24, 73

Deifell, J., 39–40

Deupree, R., 73

Disney Corporation, 74–75

Distrust, 109

Diversity, cultural, 85–86

Dominion, 130

DreamWorks studios, 68

Drucker, P., 24, 134, 151

Dysfunction, learning from, 105

E

Easum, W. M., 6, 92, 130

Ebel, S. H., 120

Eisner, M., 75